Pra

How to Get People to Scream Your Name and Beg For More

The P's and Keys to Living the Ultimate Life

This book offers insightful lessons that will change your perspective and practical advice that you can use in your daily life. Learn to use your strengths and improve on your weaknesses to be happier and more productive in your personal and professional life. Tom's energy is contagious and you will no doubt finish this book with tips you will be excited to put into practice. **Jim Wacksman, President, Association Studios**

Tom tackles life's challenges by sharing his experiences, wisdom and compassion. I enjoyed Tom's down-to-earth easy to understand prose - he uses real examples from his life. Throughout the book, you'll find the tools you need to clarify your goals and build a support system of family, friends, colleagues and acquaintances that are indispensable for your success. **Sheri Jacobs, President, Avenue M Group, LLC**

Tom Morrison has hit a homerun with How to Get People to Scream Your Name and Beg for More. With his book, Tom has uniquely given simple task lists and exercises that anyone could follow and live out. His strategies fit every age, and every genre of life. Employers should consider offering this great book to their employees, as well as their friends. Many people dream and hope for a new life, Tom's book explains how. **Tim Owen, President, Owen & Associates, Inc.**

How to Get People to Scream Your Name and Beg For More

The P's and Keys to Living the Ultimate Life

Tom Morrison

Published by Waldorf Publishing
2140 Hall Johnson Road
#102-345
Grapevine, Texas 76051
www.WaldorfPublishing.com

How to Get People to Scream Your Name and Beg For
More, The P's and Keys to Living the Ultimate Life

ISBN: 9781942749288
Library of Congress Control Number: 2015930847

Printed in the United States of America

Foreword by Richard Marks PhD, LPC

Dr. Marks is one of the country's premier experts on life, relationships and communication skills. Dr. Marks has counseled thousands of couples and speaks to small companies to Fortune 500 companies throughout the U.S. on building sound life and relationship skills that last.

Having been in the field of psychology, counseling, ministry and personal development over the last 28 years I have learned much about life. Having come from a broken home and having battled challenges in my own life, I struggled along in my early twenty's trying to find balance and success. Fortunately, some great teachers came into my life and I learned a new way of thinking and how to become successful as a man, a husband, a father, and in my vocation. The man I am today has been a composite of the inputs I received from my teachers and my willingness to be teachable.

Along life's journey people come into your life and they go. One such person I met in 1999 was Tom Morrison. Tom came to visit me as he was starting a city wide initiative to help singles find their potential and be successful in their lives emotionally, spiritually and relationally. His passion for helping others was infectious. I would sit back and marvel at this man (who became a friend and an encourager to me personally) who could inspire not only individuals but groups. As I got to know Tom personally and learned of his life's journey (and some of that I got to walk through with him) I found a man who could learn from his choices, from the things that happened to him, and overcome all of these to live out what he calls the Ultimate Life. His ability to connect with others, network, inspire, motivate, encourage and teach others is truly his gifting. And more than academic, the things he teaches come from who he is as a man, a result of living life and living by the principles he introduces to you in this his first book.

Tom asked me to read his book. I was honored to be asked and was glad to do so. Then I sat down to read it. Wow! As I was reading I could hear Tom talking to a crowd. I could not only hear Tom's heart and words in the book, but I could also picture him teaching others. This book is true to the author. It is Tom Morrison. Through vulnerability, authenticity, humility and his characteristic humor, he takes the reader into not only the various challenges people experience but applies his paradigm for success to each situation. Whether you are married, unemployed, single, a single parent, a leader or a follower, the principles taught in this book will inspire and encourage you to live and experience the Ultimate Life.

All I can say is that as I read this book I found myself screaming "YES!" I so agree. Tom has been able to capture the principles of personal development, psychology, spirituality and put them together in a simple, yet profound message. Yet it is so very practical. And after all, isn't that what we really need today? A practical and inspirational approach to living life to its fullest. By taking the time to invest in reading his insights and wisdom, and applying these simple and practical actions, I hope you find people screaming your name and begging for more of what you have.

Richard Marks PhD, LPC

Table of Contents

Dedication

I would like to dedicate this book to all the people who inspired me to put my hands on the keyboard and share my thoughts on life. These people live life each day grinding out the opportunities and challenges that come before them. Each is seeking to change their circumstances to enjoy a better quality of life, but never seem to know what path to take.

My dedication goes out to:

The person who's life is on the right track, but continues to have a deep desire to keep moving to the next level in life in pursuit of excellence.

The college student who wants a clean road to success without all the bumps that can come along the way.

The single mom and dad who are stressed, feel like their energy bucket is empty and at their wits end to get it all done.

The parents who want to provide their college age kids a good book to prepare them for what's ahead.

The couple who can't seem to get their house in order with all the stresses that come with raising and meeting the obligations of being parents.

The person who is in a bad relationship and needs to understand how to move forward to improve the relationship or get out.

The young kid in a bad neighborhood surrounded by bad circumstances and wants out to achieve the quality of life that will provide a positive future.

The person who feels that no matter what they do, their decisions push them into a deeper hole in life.

The business professional, who feels like they have it all, yet their soul and heart feel empty.

The person who is under the weight of debt and needs a path of hope.

Those in pain who are seeking to overcome their circumstances to feel the pleasure and joy life can offer so many.

Those who want to laugh more, enjoy life more and feel good about who they are each and every day.

I have written this book in your honor in that it provides you a path from pain to pleasure… from anxiety to joy… from desperation to hope.

The first step in changing your circumstances is to take the first step. Good luck in your journey towards your ultimate life.

Chapter 1
Why Do I Need People to Scream My Name and Beg For More?

"Every day people come through your life who can help you create an opportunity or solve a problem, and you choose to let them pass you by."

So you want to know how to get people to scream your name and beg for more? I will say from the onset that throughout your life, having a big network of people in all walks of life will be your #1 tool to creating success in your life. People pass through your life every day. All of them have the opportunity to have a positive impact on your circumstances. The question is, will you reach out and allow them to have that impact?

I'll actually make a challenge to you right now on the first page of this book. I want you to buy a punch counter that you hold in your hand, and click every time you speak to someone on the phone, online, or in person. This number is way more than you would ever think it is. Everyday people enter your life who have their own network of people: influential contacts, expertise, talents, and resources, and who can, at some point, help you reach your goals and obtain what I call the ULTIMATE LIFE.

Before we get deep into this book, I want you to know my life is amazing. It is amazing because of everything I have learned throughout my many ups and downs, and because of the actions I have taken from those life lessons. People look at my life now and think, "Tom, you live a great life." That may be true today through their eyes, but most don't know the path it took me to get here. You see, it hasn't always been great. I grew up in a divorced home that presented many challenges to me, and I didn't even realize it until much later in life. I didn't study well, and graduated college with a 2.28 GPA. I couldn't get a job out of college because of my GPA, and I had to bartend just to make ends meet. I've been through the pains of divorce. I've been through the painful process and humiliation of having to file for bankruptcy. I went from being CEO of a major non-profit, to working in a sub shop, just so my family could make ends meet. I've had friends join together to pay my mortgage when I didn't have the money one month. I've gone to bed on Monday wondering if I was going to have enough money for groceries to feed my family, come Friday. I've gone on interviews for jobs knowing I needed to be hired by the end of the month, or life was going to be very different for my family.

I've been in the valley, as many of you reading this book are, or have been at one time. The encouraging news for you is, I came through the other end to seize the moment and achieve the ultimate life I always wanted. When I say "ultimate life," it's not a billionaire's life…it's not a millionaire's life, not even close. I'm a regular guy, who leads a regular company that seizes every moment that I can to experience life no matter what circumstances are in my way. My goal of this book is to help you see that it's not only the movie stars and rich and famous who can live an amazing life. Regular people live them every day. I'm living proof, and I want to show you the path to creating your own ultimate life that rewards and fulfills you every day.

Now you may be asking yourself, "Tom, what is the ultimate life?" My friend, the ultimate life is an incredible feeling! It is a place that is, by no means perfect, because life isn't perfect, but you feel an amazing sense of joy, love, fulfillment, excitement, and purpose. I've seen many living on the edge of financial struggles, and if you didn't know they were struggling financially, you would think they were rich. I've seen many with everything that money can buy, but their souls are as dry as the desert on a hot day. You see, happiness and being rich aren't about how many zeros are in your net worth, what you own, or what your return on investment is.

Happiness and being rich are about the people you impact, the difference you make, and what gives you a return on life. Return on life (ROL) is a huge shift in thinking as you look at the various ways you can spend your time and money. I have seen many who build monster bank accounts and die a lonely soul. I've seen many who invest their money into making a difference in others and their life is overwhelmed with fulfillment through a sense of purpose.

Throughout this book, as you think about every aspect of your life, I want you to focus on, "What is my return on life?" as we move forward, I want you to think about a series of questions:

- Am I worthy of people screaming my name and begging for more?
- Do I bring positive or negative energy to people?
- Do people like talking to me, or wish I had never joined the conversation?
- Am I concerned with other people's lives, or am I just worried about me?

- Am I open to new innovative thinking and change for doing things, or am I caught up in the same old way?
- When I speak, do I build people up, or do I tear them down?

In my life, I have found that people treat you as you have treated them first. Your first set of comments, actions, or decisions set the stage for how people view you, treat you, and possibly help you when asked. The more people have a positive outlook about you, the more people you have at your disposal to help build and enhance your quality of life. An important step in looking at who YOUR PEOPLE are is to determine what kind of people you are attracting. YOUR PEOPLE are the people you surround yourself with on a constant basis. As you will learn in this book, YOUR PEOPLE have the most influence on who you are as a person and the direction your life takes. The answer to the questions above will help you answer the question of, "Who are YOUR PEOPLE?" If you don't like the people you are attracting, and you feel they are holding back in living the ULTIMATE LIFE, you might need to look in the mirror and make some changes in you. As you change, you will see YOUR PEOPLE change. Some will leave your life because they are unwilling to grow and change, and others will mature into a group who totally engage your life in a positive way. We will talk in depth about this later in the book.

After you have looked into yourself, you then need to figure out, "who are my people?" I have found in my life that no matter what level of life you are operating in, how old you are, what your circumstances are, or if you work for yourself or a business, if you are going to maximize your quality of life both personally and professionally, it is imperative that you have people screaming your name and begging for more.

Think about it. With the rate of change in today's environment, it is crucial that you are surrounded by a network of people who you can instantly reach out to, and who can help you achieve your goals when needed. If you work for a company, you need to have three to four companies you can call who have said to you, "If you ever decide to leave your company, give me a call." If you are ever fired for any reason, you have a place to land and protect your financial position and family security.

If you are an owner of a company, you need to have a dozen or so people who are great at what they do, and that you know would come work for you if one of your key people left for any reason. This will help protect your service to your customers and maintain the financial security to your company.

If you are a college student, you need to network with business owners and executives so that the moment you graduate, you have an immediate job to walk into. Now wouldn't that be awesome!

If you are a single mom with a job, it is an amazing feeling to have a list of people in your phone that can pick your kids up, babysit, and help you at a moment's notice. I've been a single father with young children and really feel the emotions and challenges single moms go through. It isn't easy and is a full-time job all in itself.

No matter what your mode of life, whether personal or professional, the more people you have around you who want to scream your name and beg for more, the easier and more successful your life is going to be. People are somewhat like money in that "money isn't everything, but it sure makes your life easier the more you have." People are in that context, except I would contend that people ARE EVERYTHING because they can have such an amazing impact on your life...if you let them in. That is what this whole book is about. Along your journey through this book, we are going to look inside and touch almost every area of your life to help you make the necessary changes to reach the ULTIMATE LIFE.

If you are content with your life but desire more, GET READY. If you are unemployed, GET READY. If you are a single mom or dad, GET READY. If you are unhappy with your current circumstances, GET READY. Each chapter will be filled with wisdom, insight, and stories that I have assimilated throughout my life. I've had the fortunate pleasure of having some of the most amazing mentors, business owners, and speakers impart on me powerful truths that paved the way to my incredible life experiences, happiness, and memories. At the end of each chapter, you will find exercises called, "Application to the Ultimate Life," and "Action Steps to the Ultimate Life." These are to help you think through each chapter, and put down on paper practical action steps you can implement to make the necessary changes in your life.

If you want more out of life, GET READY. Get ready for an amazing journey. Get ready to roll up your sleeves. Get ready to dig into your life. Get ready to make positive changes in your life that will carry you to the "promise land" called the ULTIMATE LIFE that is filled with joy, love, self-worth, and fulfillment.

Chapter 2
You Are the CEO of Your Life

"You have more control over your life than you think, and things are never as bad as you think they are."

As I start this chapter, I want to dispel something that many people have been taught over the last couple of decades. It is the frustration of many young people, and many adults don't want to believe it: THERE ARE WINNERS, AND THERE ARE LOSERS IN LIFE. Now, I don't mean that people are characterized as winners and losers. In the results of life events, there are winners, and there are losers. When you are out in the real world, everyone is not as good as everyone else, and not everyone gets a trophy. In the world or applying for jobs, out of ten people in an interview, only one gets hired and nine do not. One won the interview and nine lost. When there are ten proposals for a business deal, one wins and nine lose. If you are to live life without frustration, it is crucial that you understand that you are going to be on the losing end in a lot of circumstances. The question is, "What do you do with that moment of losing?" You can have self-pity and be frustrated that the world isn't fair or you can learn from those losses and choose to use it to improve yourself so you become stronger and a positive force in your life. My point is, life isn't an even playing field. It is highly competitive where you must work hard, work to earn what you desire and be dedicated to achieving your goals. Even when you give 100% of yourself in the process, you are going to lose a time or two. But if you give 100%, you will not lose nearly as much as those who aren't willing to do what it takes to achieve their goals. Two keys to live by in life are: learn how to accept loss with class and grace, and hate to lose more than you like to win. This mindset will help you to not let losing devastate your life, but to drive you to continue giving your all in the process.

So many people walk through their life with so much anxiety and fear, all because they feel out of control of their life. They are worrying about all the things that they feel they can't control, yet they are forgetting to get their hands on the things that they can control, and do those things incredibly well. You need to understand that you are the CEO of your own life. When I say "CEO," I mean the Chief Energy Officer. The buck stops with you. No one can hurt your feelings if you don't give them the control of your feelings. No one can control your life long-term if you don't allow them to. No one can make you do things against your beliefs, unless you let them. If you are allowing people or circumstances to control you, you need to find the strength and path to take back control of your life and become the CEO of your life. This book is about rediscovering yourself as CEO and living the ultimate life that you desire.

There is a saying I heard one time in a business seminar, which really is one of the key central points in fulfilling all the dreams you desire. In life at all levels, "You get what you demand, or you get what you tolerate." Throughout your life, people, your circumstances, your job, your family, and even the people closest to you, are all going to bring some chaos your way that will have a negative impact on your life. So many overlook those things by saying:

- "They didn't really mean that."
- "If you would just get to know them, you would like them."

- "It's just a phase, they will come out of it one day."
- "I know they wouldn't do anything to hurt me."
- "I know they will pay me back."

I'm here to tell you, that if you allow anyone to take advantage of you, people you never thought would do such a thing, will take advantage of you. I've seen it between friends, immediate family, employer to employee, and vice versa. If you are going to obtain the quality of life that you really want, that is stress and anxiety free, it is imperative that you decide what you will not tolerate from people. You need to draw those lines and stick to them. When people see that you are serious about those lines, they don't cross them. So you can see some examples of those lines, here are a few of mine:

- Don't ask me to put my work before my family.
- You will treat me with decency as a human being.
- Children are never allowed to disrespect or directly disobey.
- Being a hard worker isn't defined by making me work 50+ hours every week.
- Just because you are family doesn't mean you can treat me with disrespect.
- If you can't find anything good to say, don't say it to me.
- When we are in a restaurant, you will not run around

like you are in an outdoor playground.

• Don't bring drama without facts and a solution.

These are just a few of the numerous agreements that I have made with myself with regards to certain behaviors that I will not tolerate. If you set these lines for yourself, they will keep a positive balance on your life. Some of my lines may be the same as yours, and you may have others you'd like to add The key thing is to write these down and make a decision to not tolerate these behaviors, but rather to demand that people around you adhere to them. You may look at the lines I've listed and think I was a tyrant and rigid with my children. If you were to interview both of my kids, you would hear from them that I was one of the most fun and caring fathers you would have ever met. They would also tell you that I was a good disciplinarian as well, and helped them understand what "boundaries" and "consequences" meant in life. I worked diligently to make sure my kids knew where the lines were drawn between good behavior and bad behavior…respect and disrespect…what consequences would result from certain behaviors. I taught them that if your actions make others' lives more difficult, don't EXPECT anything good in return. The easier and more anxiety-free you make other people's lives, the more they will want to scream your name and beg for more!

Daily life for most is a grind, and people have enough

negative forces pulling at their life. If you inflict unnecessary conflict into it, they will almost always say "no" to your requests, or will not want to be around you very much.

Now, many of you who have changed your mind over the years from, "I want people to respect me," to "I want people to like me," are going to have a tough road ahead. People who want others to "respect them" are willing to walk away from people who cross their lines that they have agreed they will not tolerate. People who want to "be liked by everyone" chase after people who are crossing their lines, simply because they feel there is something wrong with themselves. Hear this: There is nothing wrong with you! In a lot of cases, the reason the other person isn't creating a positive environment in your life has more to do with them than it does with you. They are dealing with their own pasts and stuff in their life, and it is playing itself out against you. There is nothing you can do to fix that. Now, does that mean you ignore them the rest of your life? No, it simply means you let them know you will not tolerate certain behaviors that cross the lines of respect, human decency, and emotional bullying.

The bottom line is that people have a higher level of respect for others who have drawn some basic, good, and accepted behavioral standards for their own life. Decide what you will not tolerate and put them in your mobile device so you have them at your fingertips.

Now I want to get into what I feel is the most essential part of this entire book. I call it, The **Path to the Ultimate Life** visual. This visual has in it the keys to why your life is where it is today, and the keys to how you can make changes to pursue the life you want.

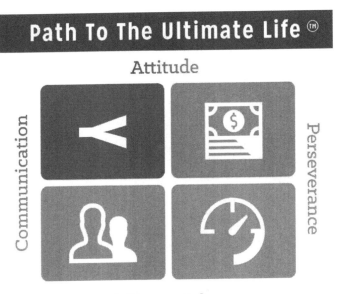

The **Path to the Ultimate Life** visual has four blocks on the inside, I will call "Pillars," and four words on the outside, I call "Characteristics." The Pillars on the inside are the four things that have the most impact on your life every day, and are the things you must do well to obtain the life you want. They are:

- Choices

- Money
- Time
- People

The four words on the outside are the four Characteristics that you must have to do the four Pillars with excellence. Those are:

- Attitude
- Ability to Adapt
- Communication
- Perseverance

I contend that if your life is not going the way you want, or if you are not getting the fulfillment out of life you want, one of the four Pillars is out of alignment in your life. Either you're not making good choices, you aren't spending your money right, you're not investing your time wisely, you're not surrounded by the right people, or you are lacking one or more of the four characteristics.

Let's take a look at each of the four Pillars and Characteristics and put them in context so you know why they are all important and interconnected.

Choices

The sideways "Y" in the top right corner box of Pillars represents the fork in the road you come to on a daily basis. Every day you make good or bad choices and warrant good or bad consequences in your life. As you continue down a road of bad choices, they tend to multiply and make things worse. Learning how to make good choices is a "mindset" of how to analyze what is good for your life and what isn't. I know many people who want to earn $100,000 a year, but aren't willing to make the good choice to go to college, or at least a two year technical school to find a high-paying trade to work in. I know others who want to own a business, but aren't willing to make the serious set of choices needed for owning a company. They just want it handed to them. I know high school students who want to go to a nice university, but aren't making the right choices to keep their GPA at a level that gets them accepted. Remember, your choices dictate your lifestyle. Make bad choices, and your life will be very frustrating. Make good choices, and your life will progress towards the life you really want.

One last thing I will say on choices is that if you do not like where you are in life…you don't like the neighborhood you live in…you don't like the weight you are at…you don't like your job, or you just don't like your circumstances, you are always just one decision and three action steps away from changing things. It's really simple to change your life. We just happen to make it way too complicated. If you don't currently like your circumstances, write down where you would like your life to be 12 months from now. Then write down the first choice you need to make and three actions that you need to take. Once you are done with that choice, write down the next decision you need to make and three more action steps. What you will begin to see is you start making small steps of progress towards improving the direction of your life. Changing your circumstances does not typically come from some grandiose plan that shakes things up. Effective change comes from making choices in small incremental steps that begin to build momentum in your life. But always remember, bad choices bring bad consequences in life, business, and relationships. If you have a history of making bad choices in your life, find someone you know who has a history of making good choices, and swallow your pride and ask them to help you change your decision-making process.

I don't care how poor you are, how empty your soul is, how bad the neighborhood is that you live in, how bad your life has become, the ONLY reason it stays that way is "YOU." YOU make a CHOICE to STAY there. You are better than that, and should want more for your life. Start making your choice and taking your three steps now and seek out the life you want NOW.

Time

The second Pillar that impacts your life is Time. Time is not an unlimited resource that you have the luxury of wasting. It is finite. There are only 24 hours in a day. You sleep, on average, seven hours of that away, work another eight to ten, leaving seven or so hours a day to invest in making your life better. Later in this book, you are going to do an exercise that is going to visually show you how much time you may have left to do what you want in life. It will be an eye-opening experience to look at this visual.

The clock is ticking every day on you, and you are either investing it wisely or wasting it. If you are coming up short on reaching the life you want, you need to analyze how you are spending your time. I know many self-employed people who say to me, "I really need some more clients to grow my business." My question is always, "How much time did you spend this week taking action steps that will guarantee that you develop new clients?" I get a blank stare because they did nothing. But the question makes them think about how they need to invest their time each week generating new business. Many high school and college students are wondering why their grades are what they are, and yet they don't spend nearly enough time studying to be able to learn what they need to excel in their classes. If someone tells me they plan to spend about five hours a week at school for a course load of twelve hours, I would say, "Get ready to be a "C" student." The average student cannot spend only one hour a night on school work and excel in the classroom at a level high enough to guarantee they get into college or a good job upon graduation. Great grades are definitely connected to the amount of time you spend outside the classroom on your schoolwork.

These are just two examples of how wasting your time will have a very negative impact on your ability to have a good quality of life. As with your choices, if you are not happy with your circumstances, and your life is not going in the direction you want it to go, you need to look at how you spend your time.

Money

The third Pillar you need to definitely address is how you spend your money. Money is attached to almost every part of your life because nothing is free. You pay for everything, in some fashion. There are a couple of key items you need to really, really pay attention to when it comes to money.

- Credit cards aren't trees with money hanging like fruit that you can just grab and spend with no thought of paying back. You will have to pay it back. Failure to do so will set back your life in interest payments and a credit score that takes years to build back up.
- Credit score is your grade that tells anyone you borrow money from what your ability is to pay them back. No matter what type of loan you are looking for, they will all access your credit score to judge your ability to pay it back. If it's low, you don't get the loan, or you pay

higher interest rates. If it's good, you get the loan, and at preferable interest rates. This is the number one financial tool you need in accessing loans of any type. Protect and monitor it regularly.

- Be cautious of debt. Debt can be a really good thing, and it can be a really bad thing. It can also be a runaway train that forces you into bankruptcy. Secured debt where you are buying an asset like a home, car, or something that you can sell if you ever had to in order to eliminate or minimize the debt, is not bad. The debt arrangements you need to be very cautious of are credit cards. Credit lines and other unsecured debt are potentially dangerous because you have no asset behind it to sell and pay it off. Debt can bring on financial pressures to your family, business, and relationships. Manage it wisely.

- Have a budget with your personal life, as well as your business life. This will help you know instantly, at any moment, if you have enough money coming in to pay for your expenses. The key to any lifestyle is to live within your financial means. If you want to increase your lifestyle, make a choice to find a way to earn more money. Don't get approved for another $5,000 limit credit card and pay $50 a month for ten years to pay for your lifestyle. It's not worth it. Budgeting is easy. Write down all of the income items you have coming in and total them up on a monthly basis. Then write down all of the expenses you incur on a regular basis and total them up. You will either have money left over or not. From here you can make the right decisions…do you need more income, or do you need to cut expenses?

Learning to manage your financial health will play a crucial role in almost every decision you make in life. Financial pressures put extreme tension on any business or relationship. Learn to manage your money well. As a good friend of mine once said, "Everything's funny when you're making money." In my long life, I would have to agree 100%.

People

The fourth Pillar I'm not going to spend very much time on here because I have an entire chapter focused on the people you surround yourself with. What I will say at this point is that who you hang out with is who you will become. If you want to go a certain direction in life and none of the people you hang out with are headed that way, you will either assume their direction or need to not make them your everyday crowd.

Attitude

Attitude is the first in my four Characteristics that you must have to reach your goals. When I say attitude, I mean you need to have a good attitude that is positive, keeps you optimistic, moving forward, and works to bring people together and find solutions. This is especially true if you are a leader. People don't go where you tell them to go. They go where you go. If you show a bad attitude, your people will have a bad attitude. If you have a "failure is not an option" attitude, your team will have a "failure is not an option attitude." Your attitude will play a big role in whether people want to scream your name and beg for more. When people ask, "Who should we get to lead this project, join the team, or promote?" They aren't going to think of the person with the bad attitude. They are going to think of the person whose attitude projects hard work, a positive attitude, and a team player. You need to check yours and make sure it represents someone that people want to help advance in life.

Ability to Adapt

Am I about to say the word "change?" Yes, I just said that. Change is the one thing that is constant in our life. If you are going to continue to grow in your life and reach new levels in your quality of life, you need to learn how to adapt and change whether you like it or not. New technologies, job requirements, and the demands on your life are changing around you every day. It is important that you learn how to adapt to those changes so the friction you feel and experience is minimized. Remember, just because you have been a great employee for years, doesn't mean you will be a great employee in the future. You may still have the same great skill set as you had before, but the environment, technology, and demands of your position changed, and you were unwilling to change with it. Because of your inability to adapt, you opened the door for someone new who has the new qualities needed to take on your position. Change is happening in job requirements, the skills needed to be an at-home mom, study for school exams, and to run a business. If you want to maximize your success in life, work to embrace change and adapt. Be a person that says, "Yes, and we could do this!" Don't be the person who looks at every idea or innovation and says, "Yeah, BUT…"

Communication

The third Characteristic you will need to be successful is an effective communication style. I don't want to steal my thunder for a later chapter, where I talk about your communication strategy…just know you need a good one. You need to work at it. Lack of a good communication skill set will minimize your success in business, friendships, and relationships with your children, spouse, and friends.

Perseverance

Throughout your life there are going to be times when it seems like a cakewalk. Other times are going to feel like you have hit rock bottom and if you go any further you could be knocking on the door of hell. Remember, life is not about a destination. It is about the journey. Things will come and things will go, including the lows in your life. You need to look at the low times in your life as an opportunity to build the strength and character that you need to do the big things in your life. Doing anything great doesn't come easy. It comes with obstacles, speed bumps, people getting in your way, and unforeseen circumstances. You need to learn that things are never as bad as we want to believe they are, and you need to focus on the things you can control to weather the storm and come out on the other side. This entire book is focused on giving you what you need to know in order to persevere through the pushback in your life, so you can achieve the ultimate life. People love to scream the name and beg for more of people who persevere. They WANT to be associated with them because that attitude is contagious, and most people need help in the area of perseverance. Be one of those people who shows others that no matter what, if you set your goals and never give up, you can achieve great success.

As you read the rest of this book, I want you to take a picture of the **Path to the Ultimate Life** visual. Keep it on your mobile device. I've placed a picture of it at the end of this chapter. As life begins to drift and you feel you are not on the right path, you need to pull up the visual and ask yourself, "What Pillars are out of alignment and what

Characteristics do I need to work on?" These eight areas will drive every decision in your life. If one or more are out of alignment, you will feel conflict, resistance, or pain in your process of pursuing your goals. Work to keep them in alignment as you build your life plan through this book. Good luck with building the rest of your life.

Keep a Picture of This on Your Mobile Device

Path To The Ultimate Life ™

Attitude

Communication

Perseverance

Ability to Adapt

Application to the Ultimate Life

For each Pillar below, write why you feel it's a strength you have or how you need to improve in that area:

Pillars

CHOICES

TIME

MONEY

PEOPLE

For each Characteristic below, write why you feel it's a strength you have or how you need to improve in that area:

Characteristics

ATTITUDE

COMMUNICATION

ABILITY TO ADAPT

PERSEVERANCE

CHAPTER 3
Who Are "Your People?"

*"Just because someone is family doesn't give
them the right to treat you with disrespect.
Friends who treat you with respect and human
decency are better to have in your life than family
who abuse the privilege of being family."*

In your life, you have two circles of people around
you. You have your inner circle (YOUR PEOPLE), which
are those "screaming your name and begging for more,"
and you have your outer circle (NOT YOUR PEOPLE),
those "not screaming your name." Being in the inner circle

or outer circle is not determined by family status, if you are a friend, or how close you may be with someone. Which circle people are in is determined by their comments, actions, and decisions made that have any impact on your quality of life. You want to conduct yourself in a way that maximizes the number of "YOUR PEOPLE" in the inner circle who are making comments, decisions, and actions that are having a positive impact on the quality of your personal and professional life.

Now you may be asking yourself a couple of obvious questions like, "Tom, why would I want people to be screaming my name and begging for more?" That is a great question. Let me clarify.

When I say "scream your name," this means being surrounded with the right people who have a passion for your well-being…your best interest, and have a desire to see you do well in life. They purposefully don't make comments, actions, or decisions that have a lasting negative impact on the well-being of your life. This isn't to say they don't ever make a hard decision, tough comment, or action that you are not happy with. If they are YOUR PEOPLE in your inner circle, generally tough issues are ones you have openly discussed and have determined that everyone is going to have to take a little on the chin. Sometimes making the right decision isn't always a happy decision. But you make the decision knowing each party has differing opinions and you each respect that decision.

YOUR PEOPLE make decisions with a level of care, trust, and respect for you.

The next question you may be asking is, "Tom, Who are my people?" That is another great question. You need to realize that you will never make it through life living on an island. People are always going to have an impact on your quality of life at some level. The question is, "When people make comments, decisions, or actions that could have any impact on the quality of your life, do they make a decision, comment, or action that has a positive impact or negative impact on you?" People tend to put emphasis on decisions made by those closest to them, like family and friends. Every day, people on your fringes make decisions without you around and those decisions have a good or bad impact on you. People on your fringe could be employees, fellow workers, customers, or industry colleagues. The way they think about you, how you conduct yourself, and how we treat them can play a major role in their decisions, comments, or actions that impact you.

YOUR PEOPLE should include family members, customers, friends, employees, or anyone who can make a comment, decision, or action that could influence the direction of your quality of life. Practically every minute of every day, people influence and impact the direction of your life at varying levels. Don't get me wrong, you cannot and will not make everyone you encounter happy, and not everyone will be YOUR PEOPLE. They have their own personal issues that they are dealing with that will prevent them from lining up with you. However, the way you conduct yourself, your energy, your attitude, the things you say, and how you treat people will work to maximize the number of people who want to be YOUR PEOPLE. Your goal should be to conduct yourself in a way that helps to increase your inner circle of YOUR PEOPLE so that you maximize the experiences, memories, and quality of life you experience, both personally and professionally.

On a day-to-day basis, there are generally five groups of people who make up your interactions. These people have consistent contact and influence on your life at some level. I have broken them down below in a graphic with a short explanation of each one afterward.

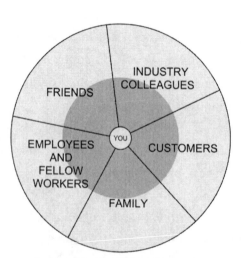

Inner Circle: YOUR People
Outer Circle: Everyone Else

Family

Family has a direct impact on your life because they are in it every day. There is an emotional bond that makes their connection with you very personal, and decisions deep-rooted. You would think that family would be the easiest people to get to scream your name and beg for more because of that personal bond. Sadly, more often than not, family can take advantage of you the fastest, or encourage you to make bad decisions because of that personal bond. Some family members know they can use the personal connection to influence you to make a bad decision because you would never think they would want to take advantage of you. I've witnessed family members borrowing money from other family members, knowing they have no intention of repaying the money. They took advantage of their family relationship and leveraged it to get the money they felt they needed for whatever purpose. Bad decision to lend the money. I've seen older parents make bad choices due to the influence of their older children, because the child leveraged their relationship under the notion, "If you make that choice, I'll never speak to you again." Never make a choice based upon this statement. Just because someone is your spouse, child, or close family member, doesn't give them the right to treat you unfairly, disrespectfully, or force you to make a bad choice. YOUR PEOPLE should never make that a condition a part of a major decision that has potentially negative consequences on your quality of life.

On the flipside, family members also make certain decisions based upon their relationship with you. As family, you get the "benefit of the doubt." Their trust and care for you supersedes their desire for you to make a bad choice. You need to understand and be able to discern between a family member looking out for your best interest or the one looking to take advantage of you so you know when to say "no," no matter how hard it is. You should say "yes" only to those family members who have your best interest at heart, not their own agenda in mind.

Friends

Friends are great. They come, they go, and like a soap opera, when you pick back up, it's like you never left. However, like family members, they can and will use the personal bond for their benefit. They will be "time suckers" if you allow them to pull you into their daily drama. Stay close to the ones whose actions, decisions, and comments align with where you want to go in life. This doesn't mean to ignore the time wasters. You need to spend time with them, listen to them, and try and help them make good choices, but don't allow them to dominate your time in their negative world. Remember the four Pillars. Time is an asset you cannot recoup. Once it's gone, it's gone. Don't waste it.

Employees and Fellow Workers

Whether you are the business owner or an employee of a company, employees and fellow workers are like your daytime family. You probably spend more time with your fellow employees on an annual basis than you do your family, given you spend eight to ten hours a day with them five days a week. It is crucial you get to know them and let them know you at some level so they will be YOUR PEOPLE. Problems at work will play themselves out at home if you aren't careful. A bad day at the office can cause a bad night at home for your spouse/partner and/or children depending on your attitude when you walk in the door. If your employees are YOUR PEOPLE, then they are working to create a positive and encouraging work environment you enjoy. Remember, home life is tough for many and if you help create a very energetic and positive environment at work that feeds their self worth, your fellow workers or employees will all want to be YOUR PEOPLE.

Customers

Whether you are an owner, sales person, or general staff, customers are a huge influence in our life. Each day, they make decisions to buy your products and services, as well as refer your company to others. As referrals and purchases go up, companies thrive, and so do their employees. As referrals and purchases decline, companies do poorly and jobs are eliminated. In my opinion, every single employee plays a role in the customer experience. It is imperative you have a good attitude and bring your best to work every day to serve your customer to make sure they are one of YOUR PEOPLE. My motto is: "Every person in a company should treat customers as if they are the only reason they do business with your company."

Industry/College Peers

Industry and college peers are huge in our process of networking, business, and professional development. Industry and college peers can refer business, partner with you on large projects, provide valuable information and resources, or connect you to someone else who can help you capitalize on an opportunity. This group of people definitely makes choices on how they interact with you based upon your integrity, how you treat them, and how you help them. When it comes to creating an awesome quality of life, this group of people plays a huge role. You will want to have a perpetual plan of increasing this group of people as YOUR PEOPLE each year. Remember, many of your friends in your industry, as well as college will rise to be presidents of companies, or very influential people who can help further your professional or personal life. I will speak later in the book on how to be a master networker.

Bottom line, every day you have a big group of people who are impacting your quality of life in a positive or negative way. YOUR PEOPLE have a positive impact on you. Everyone else has a negative or no impact on your life. Your goal should be to live your life in such a manner so as to maximize the number of PEOPLE SCREAMING YOUR NAME as loudly and passionately as possible. Doing this will maximize your life experiences, create memories, grow your financial security and increase the quality of your life.

Application to the Ultimate Life

Which group of people do you need to work on expanding in your "YOUR PEOPLE" circle?

- Family
- Friends
- Employees/Co-Workers
- Customers
- Industry/College Peers

What do you feel are your biggest challenges to expanding "Your People?"

Action Steps to the Ultimate Life

Write down the two outside influences you will need to confront in order to expand "Your People?" How will you deal with the outside influences?

What is your action item to implement in the next 30 days to make positive change and begin expanding your people?

Chapter 4
Are You a Bully or a Builder of People?

"What do people lack in their life that makes them feel like they have to bully people to get what they want? Bullies divide people. Builders bring people together."

As people enter into or pass through your life, you will always be characterized as one of two types of people: a builder of people or a bully of people. You can be seen as someone who is neither, but generally with all interactions, you are either a builder or a bully. Builders are people who have a desire to see people do well. They extend a little grace because they know life isn't perfect and neither are people or processes. Bullies on the other hand can't wait for you to screw up. You know who I'm talking about. They are the person in the meeting who always sees the glass as half empty and impresses on you how empty it is, even when you show them data that their thinking is incorrect. They are the person who emotionally beats you up in a rude fashion in negotiations. Their goal is not to have a win-win scenario, but a win-lose scenario, because they feel good when someone else feels bad. They are the person who makes cutting remarks about you, because in order for them to feel worthy in life, they must use harsh words to make someone else feel bad.

Some people have a natural part of their DNA to be a builder or bully of people. It's in their personality and what they grew up around. However, you need to look in the mirror and ask yourself, do I need to improve in this area?

So I want to ask you, "When you look at how you treat people, do you build them up or bully them around?" It doesn't matter if you are selling to customers, managing employees, babysitting kids, or trying to get your boss or parents to see things your way...how you treat people is 50% responsible for getting them to engage, be inspired, or motivated to do what you want.

If you aren't getting the things you need from people around you, you need to ask yourself the question, "How do I treat people...am I a BULLY or a BUILDER of people?" It's not the sole reason you may not be getting your way, but it plays a huge role in how people respond. A couple of other questions to ponder on this issue are:

- Do you feel you need to emotionally push people around to get what you want?
- Are you more concerned with being right, than having the right decision made?
- Are you comfortable facilitating the right decision versus being the right decision?
- What is it in your past that makes you feel like you have to bully people to get what you want?

One thing we need to understand is, life is way too hard around us on a day-to-day basis to have a boss, volunteer, fellow employee, or anyone we work with creating unnecessary conflict in our life because of something they lack. That's right. I've found in my life that most emotional bullies are that way because of something they lack internally or emotionally.

I want you to try this exercise with a friend: The next time you are with someone, have them throw an idea out to you. You both then take turns brainstorming how to make the idea better by starting every sentence with, "Yes, but..." Once you have worked through your ideas, do it again, but start each idea with, "Yes, and..." You will find that as you start with "Yes, but..." your mind can't help but think of negative things to say. On the other hand, when you do the exercise a second time through and start with "Yes, and…" you feel like you are free to explore every idea that comes to mind. You see, by simply changing two words, you were able to change your attitude within the conversation, allowing you to empower people, not tear them down.

Every person you meet, you have the opportunity to provide hope and encouragement, and create transformation in their lives. Yet, in this "feel good" state of transforming people's lives, some feel the need to bully or run over people to get it done.

- Is it because you have insecurities?
- Do you feel inferior to those you lead or work with?
- Do you feel you have to "look good" in front of your peers?
- Are there issues in your past, with parents or other relationships that are unresolved?

Hear me out on this one phrase: *"When PERSONALITIES get in the way of the PURPOSE that is the beginning of the end of the PURPOSE."* You see, bullies are more about "being right," rather than doing "what's right." Builders of people are about seeking "what's right," rather than "being right."

Knowing this, why do people continue to bully those

around them to get what they want, when it does nothing but serve the purpose of tearing apart a potentially amazing idea or team? A couple of questions I always ask people about themselves are:

- If a small group of people see you coming down the hallway, do they look to scatter before you get to them for fear of your wrath? Or, do they hang out because they want to have a moment of your time knowing you will provide positive energy in their life?
- When people leave your presence, do they feel better or worse about themselves?
- Do people feel lifted up or stressed out the moment you enter a room with them?

Don't get me wrong, there is a time to be firm, but to be a bully at every turn does yourself, those you lead, work with, or hang out with, a big disservice. Being a bully divides people. Being a builder of people brings people together.

When trying to think of an acronym that could easily be remembered on how to treat people you connect with in any scenario, especially those you lead, I discovered this: "I **C.A.T.E.R.** to people so they will scream my name and beg for more." **C.A.T.E.R.** stands for the following:

Confidence - Impress *confidence* on your people around

you by having *confidence* in them.

Authority - Give your people the *authority* they need to get the job done.

Trust - Let your actions demonstrate that you *trust* that they can make the right choices.

Empower - Don't micromanage people. You tell them the "What" and let them figure out the "How."

Respect - Show r*espect* and allow people the latitude to fail or succeed.

I'm confident if you live by the philosophy of **CATERING** to anyone in your life, you will see an exciting team of people that will develop around you and will help you accomplish whatever goals you establish.

Keep this in mind; people want to be a part of someone's life who they feel empowers them. Bullies get in the way of empowerment and create no positive progress for anyone. BUILDERS of people drive empowerment and make people's lives feel worthwhile, to the point that they will want to do anything for you.

Throughout this book, you will learn the keys to living your life, how to treat people fairly, and how to network with them to be a builder of people…not a bully.

Remember, PEOPLE are one of the keys to you

obtaining the ultimate life. If you want people to scream your name and beg for more, then you need to be a BUILDER of people.

Application to the Ultimate Life

If you are honest with yourself, do you build people up, or are you a bully? Why?

What makes you want to bully another person?

Do you feel it's okay for someone else to be right and you wrong?

How do you feel in a disagreement of any type, when someone tells you new information that you weren't aware of and which proves you wrong? Do you admit to being wrong and engage in positive dialogue? ...Or, do you continue defending your position and create undue stress in the conversation?

Are you negative to people just to be negative and get under their skin? If yes, why?

Action Steps to the Ultimate Life

At your next meeting with friends or co-workers, try the "Yes, but"/"Yes, and" exercise.

Write down three ways that you can change your attitude, words you say, or actions toward people that will make you a better builder of people.

Chapter 5
The Stages of Your Professional Life

"Two things that will hold you back in life will be comparing yourself to others, and the inability to be content in your current stage of life. Love who you are, be content with where you are, while striving to improve your quality of life."

One of my biggest desires in writing this book is to share my journey towards achieving a great quality of life and what I feel are the keys to success in everyday living. I've talked to many people who have read books or attended keynote speeches by billionaires like Donald Trump, Bill Gates, and Warren Buffett, on the keys to success. Most people listen in, but they tune out how to apply those keys to their life because they feel those people live in a "dream world," and they can't relate to their life. Only a small percentage of people ever achieve the "dream world" level of life, where financial pressures are not a day-to-day concern to them. I wanted to write this book as a "regular person," working in the "real world," to inspire other everyday people on how to have that same energetic, rewarding, and fun-filled quality of life I've been able to experience.

I once gave my son a card for his birthday that read, "Life isn't about money. But it sure makes life easier." The more successful you are in your professional career or business, the more freedom and opportunities you will have to experience life personally and with your family. You don't have to be a millionaire or billionaire to experience the best in life.

When you look at your professional career or business life, there are nine stages that everyone fits into at any given point in time. I will outline these nine stages in just a bit, but if you are like most, you are in pursuit of moving up to the next stage throughout your life, to increase your financial opportunities or resources.

Do you remember the best advice you ever received from someone? Advice that spoke into your soul that allowed you to breathe and say, "Life is going to be OK." I can remember mine like it was yesterday. I was the ripe old age of 19…full of life and energy, in the middle of taking a semester off from college to relax, after 13 years of being in school, and I was one of the top bartenders at a major entertainment complex in Orlando, Florida. I loved bartending because it taught me everything I needed to know about communication skills and meeting people's needs. Each day, I had the opportunity to mix, mingle, and converse with everyone from homeless people looking for a glass of water, to high-flying Wall Street financial planners enjoying happy hour, to millionaires waiting to meet with the owner. As I struck up conversations with each person I met, I would seek to tap into their knowledge…especially those who looked like they had achieved some sense of success and lived a good quality of life. Those that I perceived had the type of success that I was looking for in my life, I would ask for their best advice for a 19 year old in college.

The #1 piece of advice came from a man who owned his own company. I chatted with him a fair amount throughout the night, laughing and enjoying some great conversation. At the end of the night, he knew I was serious about wanting to be more than a bartender and he asked me to come to the end of the bar for a few moments. When I got to the end of the bar, he put his arm around me and gave me some of the best advice that I still live by…even today. He proceeded to share with me that life happens every day whether you show up or not. He stated, *"Life is a long ride. As a 19 year old, don't be in such a hurry to get to your destination without enjoying the ride. Pick your pace of life that is comfortable with the lifestyle that you want to lead. Don't be in a hurry to get to success. If you work hard, surround yourself with good people, and don't burn bridges, success will come. Set goals that are specific enough to keep you focused, but general enough to be flexible to seize the opportunities that come out of nowhere. Don't ever assume that you cannot do a job. We are always more talented than we want to believe."* I thanked him for his advice, shook his hand, and said good night. This man never really knew the impact that those short 5 minutes meant to my life. I let what he said sink in, and the whole week following I began to think about my future related to the statements he made:

- Setting goals that are specific enough to keep you focused, but general enough to seize opportunities that may come our way.
- Don't be in a hurry to arrive at the destination of success. Enjoy the journey along the way to success. After looking at my life and where I wanted to be in the future, I set the following specific goals:

Goal 1:

I wanted to graduate college by the time I was 25. I was in no hurry to graduate. I was going to work for the next 50 years of my life with not nearly as much freedom to enjoy life as I did as a college student. Why graduate at 22 and jump into a career that would demand so much of my life so soon? I wanted to work on being me, and enriching my life instead of serving a boss. I figured the better and more mature I was coming out of college, the better and more mature I would be as a professional in the workplace.

Goal 2:

I wanted to get my first career job out of college by 25 and work there for five years. As I studied employment ads for management at 19, I noticed that all of them wanted five years of management experience. If five years was the magic number, then I wanted to land at a company after college and stay there five years to get the best, real world experience to match up with the knowledge I had learned in college. Along with getting my first job, I had a desire to find a wife and start a family. I liked the idea of having children in my twenties, because once they were off to college, my wife and I would be in our mid-forties, and still young enough to enjoy life with our kids as young adults.

Goal 3:

Noticing that there was a pretty big pay jump for those who had a college degree and at least five years of management experience with the same company, I wanted to land a job opportunity that could accelerate my financial opportunity significantly by the time I was 30.

Goal 4:

I wanted to work for 10 years in my career, and do it with such excellence, that when I turned 40, I would be able to step up to another level and boost my financial opportunity and professionalism again. I viewed this job as my last job in life…one that could carry me into my retirement years…lasting a good 20 to 25 years. During this ten-year period, I wanted to be successful enough at what I did professionally, that one day I could speak professionally, and others would pay to hear my success story. As my professional career was blossoming, I had a huge desire to be the best father and husband to my family as well.

Goal 5:

I wanted to begin speaking at some point in my forties and write an inspiring book about success in life and business.

Once I had these five goals down on paper, I now had what I felt were achievable goals that allowed me to have a great balance to enjoy the journey of life, reach a destination I deemed successful, and were focused, yet flexible.

I'm sure that with goals written out like that, you are probably asking yourself, "So how did those work out for you?" Great question! I am now 50 years of age…31 years after setting those goals, and here is what my resume looks like:

- I graduated Florida State University at 26.
- I got my first career job at 25.
- I worked at my first career job for 6 years.
- I got married at 24.
- I had my children at 25 and 27.
- I leapt into my second professional position at 31, which doubled my financial opportunities.
- I rose to the top of my industry, landing my current position as CEO of an international trade association at age 41.
- I began to speak at industry conferences at 47.
- I have written this book at 50.

When you look at my goals and the path my life has taken, it is amazing how close my path followed my written goals. Don't get the notion that it was all easy and rosy. There were numerous hiccups along the way, like divorce, bankruptcy, taking too much risk, and learning a few lessons the hard way. How you deal with that difficulty will decide how quickly you get back on track with your goals and your plan. These bumps in the road are never life-ending experiences. They are learning opportunities that help you know what not to do in the future. Not everything happened in the exact year and in the exact way I had planned, but they were pretty close, because I stayed true to the flexible timeline I had put into place. The most amazing thing about my life is that my career in association management, which I have enjoyed for over 20 years now, is one that I never even knew existed when I left college. This speaks to the part about being flexible with your goals and plans. Leave them open for unexpected business opportunity and career paths that you didn't even know existed.

The moral of the story is, "If you want to build a good quality of life in your future, you must set goals that fit the type of lifestyle you want to lead, have an executable plan to make it happen at each stage of life, and pay attention to the **Path to the Ultimate Life** visual as your guide." We will talk more about this throughout the book.

Now back to the nine stages that I mentioned earlier in this chapter. When we talk about stages of professional life, everyone is in one. Just as there are five groups of people who will have direct impact on your life day-to-day, there are nine stages of professional life. Everyone is in one of these stages at any given point in time. Following are the descriptions of the stages of life and a visual graphic:

College or Unemployed

These are people who are either furthering their education to start a career, or are not currently working.

Job Transition

These are people who are working for temp agencies, or in a job that will end due to a life change. Many college students who work in retail or food services fit this stage and then move on to the next level once they graduate.

Entry-Level Career

This is typically the first level of professional work for college students, as well as professionals starting in a new career or with a new company. The goal of an entry-level position is to get your foot in the door so you can prove your work ethic and value to the company, thereby allowing you to move up quickly within the organization.

Middle Management

This stage of life is the one that happens after you typically pass that five-year mark of experience in the company, or in leading people.

Upper Management

This stage is when you are promoted to a CXO position, like CFO, CIO, or CMO, and are in charge of many people, and have a high level of responsibility.

CEO or President of Company You Do Not Own

This stage is typically after many years of working up the corporate ladder and you are responsible for the overall executive decisions and financial success of the company.

Self-Employed

This stage fits the one-person companies like consultants, real estate agents, and personal fitness trainers. These are people who had an idea or a talent, and decided they did not want to work for anyone, so they went out on their own.

Company Owner

This stage generally happens to many self-employed people whose company grows and they have a need to hire employees to meet the demands of your customers and operations.

Super Star Dream Status

These are the "Donald Trump's," movie stars, professional athletes, and other public figures who have achieved amazing success and wealth.

Retired

This stage typically happens later in life, and is when we decide that we have enough financial resources to walk away from one of the stages we are working in above. This stage only happens to those who plan early enough in life for it to actually happen. If you don't plan for how you will have enough money in the bank "working for you" when you quit working, then your only financial resource will be social security, at about $1,000 to $2,000 a month. You will not like this lifestyle option…I promise. We will talk about this later in the book.

So which stage are you in? Do you have a desire to move to the next stage? Do you have a plan to keep you moving to the next stage? If not, you should.

Until you know where you want to go, analyze where you are, and put a plan in place to make up the difference, you will continue to spin your wheels in the same place, and wonder years later why you have made no progress.

STAGES OF LIFE
College or Unemployed
Job Transition
Entry Level Career
Middle Management
Upper Management
CEO/President of Company You Don't Own
Self Employed
CEO or President of Company You Own
Super Star Status
Retirement

Now that you have a handle on the importance of establishing some goals for yourself, and what stage of life you are in professionally, I want to conclude this chapter talking about the two things that will keep you from achieving your goals and having a rewarding quality of life.

Those two things are "comparison" and "caring what other people think about you."

I know there are people reading this book who are constantly comparing their life to others who are in a higher, more successful stage of life, and trying to play catch up. There are people reading this book who allow what others think of them to dictate way too much of their decision-making processes. They are working too hard to buy things that they don't need and to create a lifestyle to impress people who don't really care about them in a personal way. They aren't a part of "YOUR PEOPLE" as discussed in the first chapter. If you live your life constantly comparing yourself to what other people have, and let that drive your decision-making process, that will create unnecessary stress and financial pressures in your life. You will continue to work more hours, to make more money, and to keep up. Financial stress is one of the worst stresses that you can have in your life. Don't create it for yourself or your family.

I want to encourage you to be content, but not satisfied, in the stage of life where you are, and understand that you are on a journey. I firmly believe that everyone is exactly where they are supposed to be, at each stage of their life in any given moment. Love where you are, be the best in that moment, and have a desire to be moving towards the next stage of life. If you are always distracted with your destination, you will never be the best at each stage of life.

One of my life principles is to NOT be the best once I get to the destination, but TO BE THE BEST at every stage of life along the journey.

When I got my first job as a landscaper at an apartment complex in 1978, I wanted to make sure that I was the best at taking care of the complex. I loved hearing tenants say that they loved how the apartment complex looked so clean and well-landscaped. When I was a bartender in college, I strived to be the best bartender in the entertainment complex of 50+ bartenders. At one point, another bartender and I became known as the "A-Team."

As I have pursued my professional career, I have worked to be the best at my profession every single day. In 2012, I was honored by my association executive peers as the Association Executive of the Year. You see my point? You can't wait until you reach your dream job to be the best at what you do. It is imperative that you work to be the best at every stage of your professional life. Your greatness will cause people to SCREAM YOUR NAME in your next stage of life. They will recognize your character, work ethic and leadership, and will want to help you move forward. My pursuit of excellence, at each stage of my life, has been significantly impacted by people screaming my name and begging for more.

Be inspired and challenged to keep progressing forward to the next stage of life that can improve your financial resources and have a positive impact on your family and your ability to help others. You have greatness inside of you…everyone does. You just need to discover it and let it out.

Every year I see people working hard to plan for a future they cannot predict. I say, "Quit trying to plan for a future you cannot predict, and create a future you want."

Don't let what other people think about you drive your decision-making processes. If you do, you will live your life with insecurity, unhappiness, and in some cases, depression, because you'll feel like you can never make everyone happy. FREE yourself from that! Know that you will NEVER make everyone happy. Some people, because of who they are, will never like you, or think positively about the decisions you make. This is more about who they are, than who you are. Don't give them that control of your life.

What I know is that God doesn't make junk. You were created for success and you have the freedom to make success happen in your life, if, and only if, you have a deep enough desire for it, want to work hard for it, make good choices to get there, and treat people right along the way.

For the rest of this book, I am going to share with you 14 life-changing key words that begin with the letter "P." I have found that when these 14 areas of life are all in alignment, you will experience amazing levels of joy in all areas of your life. When any of them are out of alignment, conflict, unhappiness, selfishness, and bad decisions creep into daily life.

Once you have worked through the 14 "P's," I will share with you the 11 keys that you need to focus on to "Get People to Scream Your Name and Beg For More." The question is, do you want it? Do you want to wake up with a smile everyday...or with anger? Do you want people to help you when you call...or let it go to voicemail because they prefer not to talk to you? Do you want people to see you as someone who is a positive influence in their life, or someone who sucks the life out of them with negativity when you are around?

The great thing about today is that it can be the start of the rest of your life! If you live life frustrated and blaming others for your lot in life...STOP. It's your life...not others'.

Read the rest of this book, take action in the areas we will discuss, and finish life well. Have a desire to wake up with a smile, be a positive influence on everyone you touch, and enrich the lives of others. As I heard in a movie once..."Stop praying for a miracle and BE THE MIRACLE." Before that, though, you need to work on you. Good luck on the journey.

Application to the Ultimate Life

What stage of life are you in?

- College or Unemployed
- Job Transition
- Entry-Level Career
- Middle Management
- Upper Management
- CEO or President of Company You Don't Own
- Self-Employed
- CEO or President of Company You Own
- Super Star Status
- Retired

What are your biggest outside influences that you will need to confront in order to improve your current stage, or move to the next stage of life?
What are your biggest challenges to moving to the next stage? If your current stage is awesome, what are your challenges to making it a better quality of life?

Action Steps to the Ultimate Life

What is your action item to implement in the next 30 days to make positive change and improve your current life stage or move to the next stage?

Chapter 6
Defining Your Purpose

"Having no purpose in life is like trying to drive from Miami to Seattle with no map. You live in a constant state of, where are we?"

Webster's dictionary defines PURPOSE as "the reason for which something is done or created, or for which something exists." The key words here for you are, "for which something exists." No matter what stage of life you are in, my question for you is, why do you exist each day? The most successful and happiest people have figured this out. When I say "successful people," that doesn't equate to dollar signs in the bank. It equates to people who are experiencing a great quality of life that is meaningful in their heart, mind, and soul...they are experiencing joy, love, and happiness. A quality of life where everyone around them feels the positive energy and encouragement they bring with them every day. These people have a center of focus on why they were created, why they exist, and whom they were created to serve. The heat of a bad day at the office, or a supervisor screaming at them doesn't get them down because their "purpose in life" is much bigger than that one moment, so that moment will most likely not mean anything one week later.

I've witnessed people who have everything you could ever imagine financially, yet their soul feels empty, and no one wants to be around them. I've heard stories of rich people who had less than 50 people at their funeral, and a janitor who had over 500 people attend their funeral. Which of these two people reached the most people for good in their life? Which one had the most people screaming their name and begging for more?

Being rich and successful is not about a number, it's about the legacy you leave between the day you were born and the day you pass on. Oh yes, you are going to pass on. The question is when, and how do you want your life to be remembered?

To help give you some focus on you finding your purpose, let's do a little life assessment. The following is a picture with 78 squares in it. These squares represent the average life span of a person living in the United States. I want you to take a pencil or pen and color in the amount of squares that represent your age. For example, if you are 56, color in 56 squares.

Life Block Exercise

Color in the number of squares of your age

Those not colored are what you have left to live

Once you have colored in the squares, I want you to stare at that picture and realize that the colored portion is what you have lived in life. The white squares are what you have left to live. Some questions I want to ask you at this point as you stare at this image:

- Are you satisfied with what you have done do far?
- Are there people you need to forgive to be free?
- Are there people you need to ask forgiveness from for your actions?
- Does your soul feel fulfilled at this very moment?
- How would the closest people to you describe you to others if you weren't around?
- Are there things stored up in your heart that you need to say to your parents, children, spouse, or friends?
- What is on your bucket list?
- What are you going to do with the time you have left?

As you think of those questions, let me add something to the equation: what happens when you go to the doctor and receive a diagnosis that instantly colors in every block but one? Don't say it can't happen to you. It happens every single day to people everywhere. Every day, people young and old are diagnosed with cancer, have an unexpected heart attack, or are involved in a serious accident. In that moment when they come to find themselves in a hospital bed, life becomes real…and so does death. You wish you had done more. You wish you had forgiven someone. You wish you had said some things to those closest to you. You wish you had taken that trip. You wish you had...

Don't be someone who "wished they had." Start being a person today who seizes every day as if you only had one block left in the graphic above to fulfill your dreams. Be the person who writes their bucket list down and pursues it. Be the person who sees people as human beings who need help, and be there to help.

Having a life purpose gives you a central target to which all of your life circumstances point. There is a "reason" for each moment in your life. People without purpose wake up in the heat of battle and wonder "why am I doing this?" Those with a purpose know why they are doing this, and there's a huge difference in the attitude by which you live.

Everyone needs a purpose in life. Purpose provides you with focus. It provides stability. It provides an answer to the question that everyone asks at some point in their life, "Why am I here?" In my opinion, everyone has been born with a certain set of talents and passion to help serve a specific set of people or cause in their life. If you don't think PURPOSE is a big deal, then why do so many people reach 40, 50, even 60 years of age and look back at their life asking themselves after all that time, "What has my life meant? Why was I put here? Would it even matter if I disappeared?" It's crazy to have seemingly wasted all those years before you began to seek out your true purpose in life. It's why I strongly encourage all young people reading this book to define your purpose while you are at the beginning of adulthood. Purpose brings strength to your career, business decisions, as well as every personal relationship.

Don't get me wrong, if you are over 40, you haven't wasted all those years, but it can sure feel like it if you wait until after 49 to start thinking about, "Why am I here?" No matter what your age, the time is NOW to figure it out.

If you lead people at any level, when those you lead know you have a purpose, it gives them a confidence in you because they know there is stability there. They know you have direction…that you aren't just making decisions on a whim. They know you have an inner strength circled around a central purpose for your life.

I can remember when I discovered my purpose. It was January 1995. I was on my knees beside my bed in some sense of panic, emotional pain, and anxiety. I was trying to make sense of and figure out where my life had disappeared to. I was 31 years old, and a year ago that month I had a great family, wife, children, church, and job. I was living what I thought was "the dream," but as the year progressed, it all began to come apart. My wife asked for a divorce and my employer let me go. Overnight, within a year, my wife was gone, I was separated from my kids, I had no job, and I had financial obligations of child support and credit card debt that I thought I could never pay off.

As I was on the floor beside my bed in deep emotional pain, I was trying to make sense of everything. I kept second-guessing myself. I questioned everything about myself, and wanted to know how everything that was so good could go so bad inside of a year. What was my existence? Why was this happening? The pain I was experiencing was immense. When looking at my situation, I knew one thing for sure- I didn't want anyone I came in contact with in my life to experience that same pain. My life purpose was born that week.

My purpose became…to encourage and engage people in a conversation about their life to help them reach their maximum potential, and to motivate them to live a deeper and more rewarding life free of emotional pain.

I wanted to dig into people's lives at all levels to get to know their story. As I heard pain in their lives, I wanted to see how I could help to encourage them through my experiences, or to turn them to someone who could help them. What I learned is that, most times people just need someone to listen to them. I have lived this out in full force since I was 31, and love every chance I get to sit and listen to someone's story, to this day.

I want to encourage you to look into your soul and find your purpose in life. If your life doesn't have any worries in it, or you are young and have never thought about your purpose in life, don't wait until the rug is pulled out from underneath you in life to start asking the serious questions, "why am I here?" Start asking them today so your life can be more fulfilling.

If you are in a set of crazy circumstances like a failing marriage, financial issues, challenges with children, or work-related issues, then start thinking about your purpose today. Once you find your purpose, all of your challenges will begin to have clarity and a path of solutions will become visible. I'm here to tell you that you can be better than where you currently are…you can rise above your circumstances to be so much more, and you can begin to truly experience fulfillment in life and work. You can achieve the ultimate quality of life on a day-to-day basis if you take the first step and define your purpose in life.

So my challenge to you is to define your purpose this week. Here are a few questions to contemplate as you look into your soul for purpose:

- What brings the most meaning to your life?
- What people do you love to serve?
- What cause do you feel deeply connected to and want to help?
- What life experiences have you had that have prepared you to serve?
- What gets you excited when you see the progress?
- Where do you feel the most rewarded when it's accomplished?

- What gifts and talents do you possess that could help others?

Remember... purpose isn't about serving yourself...it's about serving others. As Zig Ziglar said, "If you help enough people get what they want in life, you will get what you want in life."

Whatever it is, figure it out today. It will change your life forever and make every day a great day no matter how bad life seems to get. Stop blaming others for where you are in life. Don't give your circumstances or other people control over your emotions or life. Take control of your PURPOSE today.

Once you define your PURPOSE, nothing can shake your character, your emotions, or your strength.

Application to the Ultimate Life

What keeps you from defining your purpose in life?

What brings the most meaning to your life?

What people do you love to serve?

What cause do you feel deeply connected to, and want to help?

What life experiences have you had that have prepared you to serve?

What gifts and talents do you possess that could help others?

Action Steps to the Ultimate Life

Write down your purpose in life.

Chapter 7
Discovering Your Passion

"It doesn't matter what age you are, what stage of life you are in, or how much money you have, EVERYONE has a passion burning inside of their soul."

One thing I know in life is that people love dealing with other exciting and positive people. Exciting isn't about jumping up and down, screaming, and having crazy emotion all the time. Excitement is about a life giving-off positive energy that makes people feel good about themselves. In life, you either build people up, or you tear them down. People with energy and passion penetrate the hearts and souls of others. They bring life to sad people. They give life to those not feeling worthy. If you want people to scream your name and beg for more, discovering and living out your passion is a must.

Every day, people wake up in a fog. They are people who are simply going through the motions of life, waiting on something to trigger their inner soul and passion…to motivate them to step into everything that life has to offer them. They are waiting to find the right person…waiting to have enough money to have a child…waiting on the right job…waiting for the kids to grow up so they can date one another again…waiting on the right time to retire…waiting, waiting, waiting… Waiting on WHAT?

All the while YOU are waiting, your life is passing YOU by. You wake up one day, look back, and realize that you have just wasted two years, five years, and sometimes more…waiting. Waiting for WHAT? What are you waiting on?

You go through life each day doing the same mundane tasks. You get up...if you have kids, you get the kids off to school…if you don't, you sleep a little later…you go to work...you come home...you do chores around the house...you eat dinner…you go to bed...you get up, and repeat. This mundane activity ultimately drives you crazy over time. One day, you wake up years later and feel like you have wasted years of your life with no passionate energy that gives LIFE to your life.

So many couples lose their marriage because they become bored with one another. This is how affairs start. Two people in different marriages innocently start talking about their boring lives, and next thing you know, they're sharing things that bond them emotionally. That emotion connects them in a way that, at some point, drives them to cross the line in their marriages. Why? Because of the intense excitement of their bond. Don't wait until the kids grow up. That's 18 long years or more. If you are married, you and your spouse need to find your individual passions in life, and start living them out around one another. That alone will create more excitement than you could ever imagine. There is something sexy and exciting about engaging a person to talk about their passions, and watching them in pursuit of them. They become interesting and their energy flows into your soul. Don't let someone else capture your spouse or significant other's smile with their life's passion. Discover yours, and capture their heart with it...all over again.

Many people switch jobs because it is no longer challenging. It pays well. You could do it in your sleep, yet you want to move to another job for a new challenge. Why? You have been blessed with a job that you can do in your sleep because you are excellent at it, and because you do it well, you are off at a reasonable hour and don't carry the stress of work home...because it's done. You are FREE to enjoy everything else life has to offer you, don't let your

job be your sole purpose for existence in life. Discover
your passion outside of work and make that your challenge.

It doesn't matter what age you are, what stage of life
you are in, or how much money you have, EVERYONE
has a passion burning inside of their soul. It's the cause,
group of people, or thing that gets your blood flowing…it
drives your emotions. Your passion is that place where, if
you could be a part of it and not get paid, you would do it
in a heartbeat. However, if you could get paid to do it, how
cool would that be! For some, their passion is children…for
others, it's animals…others, it's the environment…others
still, it's cancer, heart disease, or the elderly. What's yours?

My passion is people. I love people. It fits right into
my purpose discussed in the previous chapter. For over
twenty years I've worked in executive management for
non-profit trade associations. One of the most amazing
reasons I love working for an association is that it provides
me an open forum to make a difference in people's lives. It
allows me the opportunity to help them transform from
going nowhere in life, to heading in the direction of their
dreams…from feeling pain, to feeling the pleasure and
excitement of living out their passions…from being angry
and hurt, to being happy and whole…from feeling like they
aren't worth much, to knowing they are worth it all.

Living your passion isn't about waiting until you have
the time to pursue or finance it. It is about discovering what
it is and starting in the pursuit of it…NOW…like TODAY!

I can remember when I got to live out my passion at an extremely high level in my mid-30's. Granted, I have lived my life with passion for the last 20 years as CEO of three different non-profits, but the second one is an amazing story of how I took a leap of faith to pursue my passion and chase my dreams.

It was 2001, and I had just left my first trade association in Orlando, Florida, to move to Jacksonville so I could be near my two children, who had moved there a few years earlier through their mom's second marriage. I had started an online fundraising business circled around online auctions, and it was beginning to build momentum when 9-11 happened. As with many small businesses, mine was a casualty of 9-11, in that my business model depended on companies to donate items for online auctions to benefit non-profits. Once 9-11 occurred, companies wanted to give most of their charitable contributions towards the 9-11 cause, and my business went by the wayside.

With a "never give up" attitude, and needing a job, I proceeded to market myself around Jacksonville, Florida, for CEO jobs in local non-profits. It's what I knew best and was very good at. Over the span of a year, I interviewed with numerous companies. Eight times I made it through hundreds of applications, numerous interviews, and made it to the final two. Eight times that happened! All eight times, they went with the other candidate. I couldn't believe it. I was told each time that the other person had an intangible edge that they felt like they needed to go with.

The one lesson I want to share with you right here is, "Passion breeds perseverance." When you are passionate about who you are and what you want to do in life, nothing can get in your way. It is just a matter of time before everything lines up, and BAM, you are living it out.

After being denied eight different times for executive positions, my decision to take the leap to pursue my passion on another level came on the front porch of a friend's house. The year before I moved to Jacksonville, I attended a weekly gathering of over 1,000 single adults called Orlando Metro. It was a weekly event where singles could come into a healthy environment, listen to an amazing live band, hear a life-giving message on life skills, and meet new friends. Over the year I attended, my life swelled with joy, my network of positive friends grew by ten-fold, and my life was transformed. When I moved to Jacksonville, I put a two-page executive summary together for an Orlando Metro concept in Jacksonville, called JaxMetroLive. That executive summary sat on my desk until after I had been passed over for a CEO job for the eighth time.

I was on the front porch with a friend, enjoying a chilled beverage, on the night of coming up short for the eighth time for a major position. My friend and I were chatting and laughing about how crazy it was for me to make it past hundreds of applicants, multiple interviews, only to come up the number two choice eight times. That's got to be a record somewhere.

My friend looked at me at one point, knowing my internal desire for my JaxMetroLive concept and said, "Tom, instead of interviewing people for a job, why don't you interview people for money to start JaxMetroLive?" My heart started pumping, my adrenaline started running, and my mind started racing. I couldn't believe what he had just proposed to me. I immediately said, "That is an amazing idea!" That night I lived out and did what I preach to everyone…sometimes you just have to make a choice to pursue your passion and run after it. So I did.

I immediately started networking around Jacksonville to find the movers, shakers, and funders for people like me with an idea that could change people. Within a few months, I had a major contribution from a well-known businessman for startup costs and another one hosted a fundraising dinner for me. I had a major facility, with state-of-the-art meeting space, offer to host the weekly event for free, a very talented band came on board, and a nationally known speaker on relationship skills signed with us to help us reach the singles community in Jacksonville. All of this happened within a five month span. It was crazy how everything we needed just came to me.

When JaxMetroLive hosted its first event, it drew in over 300 people. By week three, we had over 600 people coming every Thursday night to hear amazing live music,

life-giving talks, and networking with others through the
challenges and opportunities in life. It was powerful. I was
living my purpose and passion every day…engaging the
lives of thousands of people from as far as an hour away, to
help them know that there was more to life than their pain
and their past. Over the three-year period of JaxMetroLive,
we saw people who were running a bad path of life on
drugs, alcohol, bad decisions, and horrible pasts, to find
purpose in their life, self-worth, and a path to living the
ultimate life. Every email or conversation I had with people
about their changed life made my heart swell with joy.

I share that story to illustrate that your passion is just a
choice away. It's one step away from becoming a reality
for you. That is not to say that you need to quit your job, or
run off on some tangent in life. You need to be smart about
your choices, but you could be closer than you think to
embarking on the journey of living out your passion.

I've been working in association management since
February 20, 1995. I remember day one like it was
yesterday. Every day has been an incredible journey. It
hasn't come without its set of challenging moments, but
when your purpose is in place and you are serving in your
area of passion, challenges are always seen as
opportunities, not obstacles.

If purpose gives you a direction, then passion is what
defines you. It's what gives you energy every day because
you are working or serving in an area that creates an

emotional excitement in your life. What you are passionate
about is what causes you to take ACTION and energize
your life. My questions to you, with regards to discovering
your passion, are:

- What are you accomplishing with your life?
- What gets your blood boiling?
- What do you care about?
- What people would you like to serve/help?
- What would you do if money were no object?
- What would get you excited every day to get out of bed?
- Who would you help every day for no pay, just because
  you love it?
- What is your hobby?

Some of mine are: I LOVE playing drums...it drives
my emotional high. I LOVE dancing to 70's and 80's
music...it makes me feel good physically. I LOVE speaking
to groups of people on life and association management. I
LOVE seeing them write down action steps to help them
transform their lives. I LOVE making videos that share
stories of how associations are making a difference in
people's lives. Bottom line...I LOVE PEOPLE and I LOVE
HELPING THEM achieve success.

If you are like me, then you like to see an example of
what things look like, especially when you are looking to
design your own plan of action from scratch. For your

reference, here is what my purpose and passion statement looks like:

Tom's Purpose Statement

My purpose is to engage people in conversation, network, and connect them with others, to help them reach their maximum potential, and to live a deeper and more rewarding life.

Tom's Life Passion:

Seeing people go from, "I'm struggling" to "I LOVE my LIFE!"

Make a commitment today to design your Life Passion Statement and live it out. Someone out there needs your passion in their challenging life. You won't regret making the choice and taking that step.

Application to the Ultimate Life

What keeps you from pursuing your passion in life?
What is the one cause you have a passion for?
What people would you love to help?
If you were guaranteed a comfortable lifestyle, what would you do that would feed your soul and make you feel the most reward?

Action Steps to the Ultimate Life

Write down your passion statement.
Write down three steps that you must take to begin to live
out your passion in life:

1.

2.

3.

Chapter 8
Deciding Your Principles

"Your principles will be what you are remembered for. It's what you stand for, and the legacy that you will leave behind with your kids and grandkids."

Now that you have engaged your thoughts about defining your Purpose and discovering your Passions, the third element to living the "ultimate life" is to decide what Principles you are going to live your life by. Webster's dictionary defines Principles as: a fundamental, primary, or general law or truth from which others are derived, a fundamental doctrine, a personal or specific basis of conduct or management, or a guiding sense of the requirements and obligations of right conduct.

The key words in the definition are: truth, personal, conduct, guiding, requirements and right conduct.

You see, your principles are what guide your conduct, your heart, and your beliefs, which speak to your character and integrity. Principles are the road map for how you will go about accomplishing anything in your life. They will determine the types of people you will surround yourself with, the type of actions you will take, and how you make key decisions. More importantly, it will drive whether or not people want to interact, do business, and associate with you.

When people look at you, what kind of principles do they see in you? When you are walking towards people in your company, what are they thinking about you as you approach? How do you make people feel as you approach them, without even saying a word?

The principles people see in you drive what they think about you, and how willing they are to help, trust, and associate with you. If people do not think you are trustworthy, you will have a hard time finding people willing to help you. If people see you as a "user of people," you won't find people willing to step out on a limb for you. If people don't see you as a hard worker, they will not be willing to jump on your team and work hard for you.

The key Principles in your life can be discovered by asking yourself:

- Who are my biggest influences?
- What do I believe in the areas of trust, truth, honesty, ethics, integrity, work ethic, and friendships?
- What do I expect from other people?
- What are people's perceptions of me?
- Do my actions match up with my beliefs and what I say?
- Am I doing the right things when no one's watching?
- Who do I go to for advice?
- What books do I read to strengthen what I believe in life?

One of the most comforting emotions in life is the confidence you have when someone says something and you can take what they say to the bank because their actions always match their words. It breeds confidence in the workplace as a leader, in relationships as a partner, in children as a parent, and especially in friendships.

I've seen one lie destroy a ten year friendship. I've seen people fired over dishonesty. We have all seen marriages broken over mistrust. Your Principles dictate how everything takes place in your life. The question you should be asking yourself is, do your Principles align with your Purpose and Passions?

When it comes to my Principles, I take them from the Bible. The Bible has over 2,000 years of proven truths and life skills for every aspect of your life in relationships, parenting, friendships, how to deal with difficult circumstances, and even business relationships.

When seeking where to draw your Principles from, you need to make sure they have a foundation of being positive and successful for anyone with those same principles. Look at the lives of the people who live by those principles and ask yourself, "Do the principles they live by and stand for take them in a positive direction in life?" If the answer is no, then you need to steer clear of those principles.

Whether you are a spiritual person or not, it is critical in your life to define where you get your principles from, define them, study them, practice them, and then live them out.

Over my life, I have developed some sound principles that have helped me in every aspect of my life that I believe you would want to pay attention to. These will help you miss some of the potholes on the road of life, per se. The following are my top twelve key principles that have helped me persevere and obtain the ultimate life:

Failure Is Not an Option

If "quit" is in your vocabulary, you will always come up short in life in any area. Whether it's business, marriage, college, or any other aspect of life, you need to know that if you choose the right purpose, path, and people for your decision, you will succeed. Remember, achieving great things in life are never easy. They usually come with a bumpy road, unexpected twists and turns, as well as some push back. Almost every idea ever created was not created just by the person who patented it or actually pulled it off. Nearly every idea was thought of previously by many people; however, only one person, or a small group of like-minded people, pulled if off because of their tenacity, perseverance, and a desire not to fail. If you want to be on stage, you need to know you belong on that stage. If you want a certain degree in college or a certain job, you need to know you "own" that degree or job. If you want to climb Mount Everest, you need to know you can "own" that mountain. So many quitters were five minutes or one more key decision away from having their desires and dreams come true…but they stopped short and walked away.

I love a quote in *A League of Their Own*, a movie about the development of a professional women's baseball league back during war times. As the demands of being a full-time baseball player got tough on Dottie (played by Geena Davis) she wanted to quit. As she was walking to get in her car with her husband, who had just returned from the war, the team manager, Jimmy (played by Tom Hanks), confronted her to ask her why she was quitting. She said, "It got hard and became tough." Jimmy said something I have never forgotten. He said to Dottie, "Did you think it was going to be easy? If it were easy, everyone would be doing it. It's supposed to be hard. The hard is what makes it GOOD."

Anything worth achieving is not going to be a cakewalk. However, your perseverance will feel incredible when you accomplish your goal, and your character and strength to overcome obstacles will grow to all-time high levels. Don't ever quit on your dreams, desires, and passions…you could be one decision away from all of them coming true.

Let Go Of Your Past

(I discuss this in great detail later). This Principle is so huge for everyone, yet so many people never accomplish any of their dreams in life because of the people and experiences in their past. Some allow the past to keep them down. Others use the past as a motivator to excel. If there is someone you need to forgive to set yourself free of the past, I encourage you to do it today. If there is something you need to say to your parents to move on…do it today. If there is an experience you have buried in your soul that you need to confront, or something that needs to be said to someone…figure out how to do it soon. People lose decades of their life holding on to their past, and it just isn't worth it. Do whatever it takes to heal your past. Seek a professional counselor, a mentor, or a life coach. Sometimes just talking it out is enough to get it out of your soul. I've personally seen the past strip some people close to me of as much as 25 years of their life before they finally said, "I don't want to live like that any longer."

What is in your past that is holding you back? An abusive parent? A bad relationship? Friends who have betrayed you? Addiction? Whatever it is, get it out starting today! Get help, take action, set goals, and then GO FOR IT!

Treat Others First How You Would Like To Be Treated

In my lifetime, I have found that the people you surround yourself with treat you how you have treated them first. If you continually treat someone with love, respect, and decency, and they do not do the same to you, then they have something going on within their own life, and they are never going to be a person who screams your name and begs for more. They will always be a negative force in your life that tears down your spirit. Should you ignore them and never hang with them? Of course not. I have many people I hang with occasionally who are in this frame of mind, but they are NOT a part of MY PEOPLE that I know and can count on to be a proactive part of my life. I still treat them with respect, love, and decency when I'm with them, but I don't let them waste my valuable time with their negativity, and you shouldn't either. To live the ultimate life, you must minimize the time wasters and drama builders in your life.

Be the Change

I'm sure you have heard the saying many times, "If you continue to do things the way they have always been done, and expect different results in your life, then you are going to drive yourself crazy.

Because of technology, everything in life changes at such a rapid speed. To be successful in both personal and business life, it is critical that you embrace change; some change will be an exciting fad, others will be permanent. You need to be able to discern between the two so you can make shifts to react to permanent change. Making these shifts will help you to enhance your quality of life, and maximize your business opportunities. Those who thought Facebook, Uber, and Zillow were fads, are now operating at a disadvantage in business because they aren't taking advantage of technology shifts that could help make their life easier, and business more profitable. There are shifts in many areas like, how you can invest, communicating with people, transportation, etc. Change is all around us, and happening all the time. If you ignore it, you will fall behind and lose the opportunity to maximize the number of people who can scream your name and beg for more. Later in the chapter on networking, I'm going to share why everyone should be an active user on social media.

Managing Is About the Process, Leading Is About the People

This is a principle that is the most misunderstood principles on my entire list. The key to this principle is understanding that when you are in management, you are in charge of the process…the technical portion of the strategy. You engage in the day-to-day operations, and you are working closely with your people to get things done. If you are in leadership, the key acronym you need to know is "GOOTW." This stands for GET OUT OF THE WAY. If you want to be an effective leader, you need to make sure that you communicate clearly to those that you lead, the "What," and then let your people take care of the "How." If you want your team to maximize their creativity and output, you need to communicate the goals and expectations, then empower them and get out of the way. From there, you check in at points in time to ensure "strategically" that the team is on target. If they are, get out of the way…if they aren't, identify the gap, how to close it…and get out of the way. I have found that when you empower your team and give them ownership to use their talents and ideas, their output in anything far surpasses your expectations, instead of you dictating everything.

Don't Judge A Book by Its Cover

Every day you will meet people. Know that each of those people has a past, a personality, a story, and reasons why they may look like they do, act like they do, and think like the do. You may see people with tattoos dressed a certain way, or in a certain financial situation, and make pre-judgments about them. …wrong way to think. Never judge someone until you have had a chance to meet them, talk to them, and get to know their story. If they are in the midst of a struggle that is causing their negative outlook on life, you may be the one person who may speak encouraging or empowering words into their life that helps their life take a powerful turn. Many people on the inside are not what you think they are, because of what we see on the outside. What gives us the right to make assumptions about people based on what we see?

I can remember in 1998 I had two of my employees needing to take time off for six to eight weeks for childbirth and back surgery. I really needed someone to help me bridge the eight-week gap at work. I had a number of people I was considering. One of my employees encouraged me to interview her sister, who was a stay-at-home mom for 17 years. My first "judgment" was that since she was a stay-at-home mom, she couldn't possibly fit into our fast-paced business. I decided to forgo my initial judgment and talk to her anyway.

After one interview, I realized that she had all the skill sets that we were looking for. When I listened to what her day was like during the last seventeen years of being an at-home mom, she had amazing skill sets in organization, leadership, management, operations, meeting people's needs, and customer service. The bottom line is, I hired her and she ended up being one of the most effective employees I have ever had. She was so effective that I figured out that the two employees that went on leave had been dishonest with their time, leading me to think that they had a full day's work, day in and day out. The new employee proved to me that they only had a half-days work by doing both of their jobs more effectively by herself. Needless to say, she stayed with me long-term.

The keys again are to meet, listen, and understand people's stories. You would want the same respect.

If You Can't Do the Time, Don't Do the Crime

When I was a baseball player in high school, our coach hated when any of us watched a third strike go by. He would always say, "To be successful in life, you must go down swinging." He disliked us not swinging at the third strike so much, that if you were called out on a third strike, you had to run five laps around our baseball field, which was about one and a quarter miles. If you watched a third strike and tried to lobby for, "it was a bad call," my coach would always say, "Listen, if it's close enough to be called a strike, it's close enough for you to swing at it."

I tell that story for you to remember that if you are close enough to be pulled into a bad choice that can change the future of your life, it's close enough for you to be caught and carry some painful consequences. If you want the ultimate quality of life, know that cheaters are always found out, people never succeed through using drugs, trying to outsmart the law doesn't pay, and betraying your people will come with heavy consequences. You may live the high life for a while, but when you are found out or exposed, the bottom will fall out...and fast. The pain and expense of your recovery will be immense. My encouragement for you is to live your life right when you come to those forks in the road of a good and bad choice.

That brings to mind a story in my life that I hope every young person takes to heart. I was in my mid-teens and I was a pretty compliant kid, but I had a bit of an attitude, a smart mouth, and just didn't always do the things my parents asked me to do around the house. I wasn't a rebellious child off on wild excursions, but I just wasn't an agreeable teenager at times. I was like most teenagers, in that life was about me, not my people (family and friends). Everything came to a halt one day at sixteen, when I mouthed off to my father. He stuck his hand out and asked for my keys to my nice, customized Dodge van I had gotten for my sixteenth birthday. I loved that car and had so much fun with it in high school. I looked at him in dismay and I was like, "My keys to my car?" He said, "Yes, the keys to your car. We bought the car, you get to use the car, we get to take away the car for disrespect and disobedience." I knew I wasn't going to win this one, so I gave him the keys and had to get rides from my friends. My father told me, "When you can learn and have shown you can treat your parents with respect and decency, you can have your keys back."

Over the next couple of weeks I did some soul

searching, and realized a principle early in life that changed my life with people: "If you continually piss people off and make life tough on them, they will almost always say "no" to you, and will be unwilling to help you." Read that again and let it sink in, "If you continually piss people off and make life tough on them, they will almost always say "no" to you, and will be unwilling to help you."

In my room that night, I made a commitment, as a sixteen year old, to do whatever my parents asked. I cleaned my room up. I cut the lawn when needed. I was home by eleven, or called before eleven to ask for permission to be out later, and made sure they knew whom I would be with. It was all the typical things parents ask of a teenage son or daughter. What immediately started happening was my parent's lives became less stressful, they had more time to enjoy their own life instead of cleaning up after me, and they felt like I respected their house because I kept my part clean. What happened was a huge shift in how they dealt with me.

They began to say, "YES" to almost anything I asked. My trust level with them was off the charts because I was proving to them that I cared about what we had, and I wanted them to enjoy their life, so I wasn't creating unnecessary stress in their lives. Every day I see so many people creating so much unnecessary stress in people's lives because they are just not compliant and pursue the negative in everything.

In life, you have a choice in every area to be compliant or rebellious. I believe you need to have a compliant attitude with a rebellious streak that feeds your passion. Just know that if you are that person who chooses to always have a rebellious attitude with a streak of compliance, life is going to deliver push back, hard paths to walk to get to your goals, and fewer people willing to help you be successful.

People don't have to like you to live the ultimate life…they just need to respect you. When faced with the fork in the road with a decision, weigh the cost of whether it will enhance your life or cause grave consequences. Will it cause people to scream your name and beg for more, or will it cause people to shut you out and not want to help you or be there for you. It's your choice every time.

Birds of a Feather Flock Together

When it comes to the people you surround yourself with, make sure they have your best interest at heart, and are going in the same direction as you are. I will cover this area in great detail in a few chapters. The key in this area is whom you surround yourself with.

You Reap What You Sow

This principle is a combination of how you treat others, the choices you make, how you invest your time, and how much you put others before yourself. In life, you really do get what you deserve, as well as what you put into it. If you work hard, make good choices, operate with a high level of integrity, and treat people with respect and decency, then your life is going to have great things happen. That doesn't mean it will be perfect, or you won't have to deliver a firm hand in certain areas, but people will want to come together and help you.

If you make bad decisions, treat people with a negative or bully mentality, hedge the truth, and look for short cuts, your life is going to be filled with drama, push back, a lot of "No's" and a lack of the "right people" willing to help you.

If you continue to see bad things happen to you in your life, you need to look at my **Path to the Ultimate Life** visual and analyze your decision-making process. Take the time to find three mentors in your life who know your heart, want the best for you, know where you want to go, and consistently confide in them the choices you are faced with to gain their input. The best way to not make bad decisions is to talk to someone who has "been there, done that." Mentors can steer you towards a good path to meet your life goals. The key here is to have people who don't tell you what you want to hear, but people who, knowing all the facts you have given them, will give you open and honest guidance and feedback on which path to take.

Say What You Mean and Mean What You Say

This one is pretty straight forward, but so many people screw this up in life. I've had colleagues tell me about people they thoroughly enjoy working with at any level because when they commit or say something, "you can take it to the bank."

Don't say things to people that you don't mean, and don't commit to things that you don't intend to follow through on. This "double talk" will dilute your effectiveness and dependability factor to everyone around you. People want to know they can count on you…they really do. Don't be the person that people make the comment, "Yeah…he always says that." You always want to be someone that people know that they can count on.

A key in the area of communication is to know that some things are better left unsaid. Once upon a time, I can remember walking into a men's study group that I was a part of years ago. On the white board in the room there were three words that a prior group had been talking about that are important in communication: timing, message, intent. I was like, "I could have used that last night." Not everything has to be said at a specific moment. There is a right time to communicate and say some open and honest things to someone, and there is a wrong time. Make sure that what you want to say to someone has a positive impact on the situation. Have your words move things forward, not backward.

You Get What You Pay For

Cheap breaks. Cheap only works short-term. Cheap almost always needs to be fixed by those who provide quality work or products. One day I was driving and I saw on one side of the road a brake shop that had on their sign, "Brake Jobs: $19.95." Across the street was another brake shop that had on their sign, "We fix $19.95 Brake Jobs." I started laughing when I saw it because it is so true. If you want to expand your network of people who want to help you, don't beat them up to give you cheap pricing on something. They have a cost associated with doing business and in ultimately providing the level of service that you demand and need. They need to be able to charge enough to service you with levels of excellence. Now, that doesn't mean that you don't put things out for a bid periodically…I do it all the time, but I do it to keep my suppliers in check, and to let them know that competition exists. Once I get some competitive quotes back, if some are much lower than my current cost, I'll sit down with my supplier and ask them to share with me why their pricing is higher. They will either match the price with the same service, educate you that you will not get the same high level of service by going to the other company and you stay put, or you move to the new supplier at a lower cost.

The point here is, don't let price drive your decisions. It can end up costing you more money in the long run. With anything in life, whether in personal or business buying decisions, make sure you consider quality and service before pricing.

When people know you will not leave them overnight for a cheaper price, they are willing to do way more for you in the service area. Leverage that to your benefit.

Invitations + Time and Money = YES! (Every time)

I will expand on this in a later chapter, but I wanted to mention it here in my list of key principles. I see so many people who miss out on some great experiences because they just say "no" to invitations to experience life. My philosophy has always been, "If I'm invited to do something in life, and I have the time and the money, I always say, "YES." I've experienced so many spontaneous adventures in my life with friends and family by just saying, "I'm IN!"

I can remember a conference that I attended in the automotive industry in 1998. The hotel was full and I was able to go because one of our members had a friend who would let me room with him. He was a very successful man in his seventies, who was semi-retired from the business, but he liked to stay connected, so he continued to attend the annual conference. I remember us sitting in the room about to go to bed, when he spoke words that changed my life in this area. He said, "Tom, let me share some life advice with you. I'm now in my seventies. When I was young and healthy, I always said to myself, "When I have the time and money I'm going to do all these fun and exciting adventures in life. Well as you can see, I now have all the time and money I could want, and I can't do any of those fun and exciting things because of my health. Live life in the moment as much as you can." Anyone who is close to me would tell you I have lived that advice out as much as possible.

Don't let life get in the way of you experiencing your bucket list this year. Your health or other life factors could change at any moment and get in the way…experience life NOW! Remember the block exercise in chapter two? Don't wait until a whole series of blocks are wiped out instantly because of some life or health issue. When invited, say, "I'm IN!"

So there you have it. Those are my dozen principles that have guided my life. You will see these expanded on throughout the rest of the book. If you are consistently running off course in achieving your purpose, the first place to start looking is at the principles that guide your life, and how those are connected to your decision-making process. Look at your life purpose, your passion statement, and ask yourself…"Is what I believe (My Principles), going to get me to where I want to go?" If the answer is "no," then it's time to rethink your Principles.

Application to the Ultimate Life

Where do you get your life principles from?
How are your principles helping you excel in life?

Action Steps to the Ultimate Life

Write down five key principles you want to live your life
by:

1.

2.

3.

4.

5.

Chapter 9
Setting Your Priorities

"You can tell a person's priorities by looking in their checkbook and their day timer. How a person spends their time and money tells you what their priorities are."

Now that you have Defined Your PURPOSE, Discovered Your PASSIONS, Decided on Your PRINCIPLES, it's now time to get your PRIORITIES in order. PRIORITIES are the visual display of your actions, matching up with your words. In a sense, they are where you want to end up at the end of your life. It's what you want the dash to stand for between the dates when you were born and the date you pass on. It's the list of things people say you focused on throughout your life.

A couple of questions to think through at this point are, "Do you know what you want said about you at the end of your life?" Do your actions match up with what you say your priorities are?

I want you to turn back to page 69 and stare at your life in a set of colored boxes. Focus on the boxes that are not colored in. That is what you have left in life. If there are a lot of white boxes, you are still young…you have time to shape your priorities in a way that will expand your life opportunities to create the ultimate life for your future. My hope is that if you are under 30, you don't do what so many others do, and wait until you are 40+ to start thinking about why are you here and what your priorities should be. You may think you are all-powerful in your 20's and will live forever, but I have a cousin who woke up one day to his 19-year old married daughter calling him with what she thought was a painful headache. She was seven months pregnant, and within two hours of that phone call, she was in a coma from a sudden stroke-type condition. She lived on life support in a hospital for the next six weeks until the baby was able to be born without complications. The amount of people she reached over the next couple of months, as they kept her alive for the baby to be born, was more than most of us will reach in a lifetime. She was a true blessing and fortunately had all of her priorities in order at 19. Sadly, she was taken far too early. That could be you at twenty, thirty-two, forty-five or over sixty. Life can be shortened in a heartbeat. Start NOW, at your young age, get your priorities in alignment with where you want to be, and how you want to be remembered, and watch it create the ultimate quality of life that you desire.

If you are 40+, the clock is ticking and your time to engage life will begin to disappear...quickly. Before Facebook, you never knew so many of your high school classmates died prematurely due to cancer, unexpected heart attack, or some kind of accident, until you attended one of your class reunions. Now with Facebook and other forms of social media, you hear about it the moment they pass, because someone, somewhere, is posting about it on a social media platform. Think about it...once you get over 40, health becomes more of a serious issue. A change in health should not be the time that you decide to change your priorities. If you wait, you may not have the health to fulfill those priorities.

The point is, if you are a college student, don't live life in a way that when you wake up at 40, you figure out that your priorities were all wrong. If you are over 40, you need to get your priorities in order NOW. Don't wait until a doctor says the spot on your chest or the pain in your head are going to wipe the years off of your life and your time is limited.

When setting your priorities, there are four simple places you need to look to know what yours are:

- What do you spend your time doing?
- Where do you spend your money?
- Who do you spend your time with?
- What difference do you want your life to make?

You can tell people all day long the order of your priorities, but if your calendar and checkbook say something else, you are in denial about what your priorities are.

It has been said that you can tell a person's priorities and what he/she believes in by looking in his/her calendar and checkbook; that is, where they invest their time and money, and who they spend time with. This is so true. When I speak to groups on leadership and life growth, I have everyone answer the following 7 questions:

1. The following is a list of typical life priorities most people have in their life. Put them in the order you feel is important to you from 1 to 10, with 1 being the top priority, and 10 being the lowest:

- Spouse/Partner
- Children
- Other Family
- Work

- Faith or Spiritual Beliefs
- Volunteering (church/nonprofit work)
- Friends
- Personal Health
- Education
- Personal Fulfillment

2. If I were to ask your spouse or significant other to rate you on a scale of 1 to 10 on how much quality time you spend with them, how would they rate you? (10 being great, 1 being poor)

3. If I were to ask your children to rate you on a scale of 1 to 10 on how much quality time you spend with them, how would they rate you? (10 being great, 1 being poor)

4. If I were to ask the ten closest people in your life to rate you on a scale of 1 to 10 on how they see you spend your time, how would they rate you? (10 being great, 1 being poor)

5. If I were to ask your professional colleagues or employees to rate you on a scale of 1 to 10 on how they see you spend your time, how would they rate you? (10 being great, 1 being poor)

6. If we asked your spouse, children, friends, or colleagues to put the above list of priorities in order according to how

they see you spend your time, money, and who you hang out with, would the list change dramatically from yours?

7. If your next general check-up gave you one year to live, would the order of your priorities change dramatically?

These questions make you look at your priorities square in the face and get real with them. I'm never amazed at how many times I do this survey with both young and old executives, and they come back with the following:

- How many hours do you work a week: 75
- How would your spouse rate the quality time you spend with them on a scale of 10: 3
- How would your children rate the quality time you spend with them on a scale of 10: 4
- What is your top PRIORITY in life: My Family

This simple example illustrates that family is NOT their top priority, work is. Now, don't get me wrong. I know there are times when, in order to provide for the family, someone must work more than 40 to 50 hours a week to get through tough economic times, start up a business, or start a challenging, new job. This just shouldn't be the norm long-term for the sake of your health, your family, and your lifestyle.

When it comes to your priorities, most people want to assign their entire family as their number one priority. I believe you need to even have your family broken up into separate priorities. I want you to think through breaking up your entire family into three different priorities: your spouse, your children, and all other family. I want you to further think about the concept of making your spouse your number one priority, over your children and other family. Yes, over your children. That doesn't mean that your children receive any less love. What it means is you are going to put your relationship with your life partner ahead of your children. It means you are going to covet and protect that relationship, and not let anything inside that relationship that could tear it down. The reason many couples separate over time is because they let all types of distractions and people penetrate the one thing that they stood at the altar and committed to…each other. Trust me, if you make your spouse your number one priority, your kids will benefit because your marriage will live long past them going off to college. If you make your children your top priority, your marriage and relationship with your spouse will be put on hold, and when your kids are eighteen years old, you won't know who each other are, and will most likely separate. I see it happen all around me. And that's if you even make it until your kids are eighteen.

The same thing applies to your money. Many people say that education or family is their top priority when it comes to money, but when you look at how they spend their money, it says something different.

I've seen many young couples get married and say that their spouse is their top priority, but when you look closely at how they spend their time, they are still spending time out without their spouse, in places they shouldn't be, by themselves. Their spouse is not their top priority.

If your personal and professional lives seem off-kilter, off-balance, or stress you out, then your priorities are probably out of order and it is time to do some soul searching. I have learned in both my professional and personal lives that if your list of PRIORITIES are not in alignment with your PURPOSE, PASSION, and PRINCIPLES, you will experience conflict and frustration in many aspects of your life and relationships, including your family, spouse, children, employees, etc.

It is critical that you have your priorities written down and ask yourself: Do my actions demonstrate that the PRIORITIES I claim match up with my PURPOSE, PASSION, and PRINCIPLES? If not, it's time to make some changes.

Before you move on to the next chapter, take some time to really analyze your priorities. This is where the rubber meets the road. To help you make some meaningful changes toward getting your priorities in order, speak to those impacted by your priorities the most, and ask them for their input. Once you have collected input from those closest to you, make the time to take the following steps:

- Look at where you are spending your money.
- Look at where you are spending your time.
- Look at who you are spending your time with.
- Determine what difference you want your life to make.

Does the time and money you are spending have your personal or professional life headed in the right direction? Are the people you are spending your time with moving your life forward or causing it to stall?

You own the decisions of how you spend your time, money, and who you hang with. Align your priorities NOW so that they line up in an order that brings joy, excitement, and fulfillment to your life each and every day.

Investing time to make sure your professional and personal PRIORITIES are in alignment will pay huge dividends in greater bonds with your family and friends, a life that feels more rewarding and experiences that make you look back and go, "WOW!"

Bottom line...let your actions match your words, and you will begin to experience the "Ultimate Life."

Application to the Ultimate Life

The following is a list of typical priorities most people have in their life. When you look at your calendar, checkbook, and who you hang with on a regular basis, put the following priories in the order from 1 to 10, with 1 being the top priority and 10 being the lowest. Be truthful about your order. Next, you will be asked to put them in the order you would like to see them in.

_____	Spouse/Partner
_____	Children
_____	Other Family
_____	Work
_____	Faith or Spiritual Beliefs
_____	Volunteering (church/nonprofit work)
_____	Friends
_____	Personal Health
_____	Education
_____	Personal Fulfillment

How could your priorities change so that they are feeding your life joy, the life experiences you desire, and a sense of fulfillment?
How would your spouse, children, family, friends, and professional colleagues rate your priorities?

NOW, put your priorities in the order that they need to be in order to accomplish the things you stated in your PURPOSE, PASSION, and PRINCIPLES. Put them in order from 1 to 10, with 1 being most important and 10 being least important.

_____	Spouse/Partner
_____	Children
_____	Other Family
_____	Work
_____	Faith or Spiritual Beliefs
_____	Volunteering (church/nonprofit work)
_____	Friends
_____	Personal Health
_____	Education
_____	Personal Fulfillment

Action Steps to the Ultimate Life

What is one action item that you need to take in each of the following areas to get your priorities in order:

- Calendar:
- Checkbook:
- People you hang with:
- The difference you want your life to make

Chapter 10
The "Right" People

"You will become the people that you hang out with on a regular basis. Good people form good character. Bad people form bad character."

Now that you have Defined your PURPOSE, Discovered your PASSION, Decided your PRINCIPLES, and Set your PRIORITIES, it is a MUST that you surround yourself with great people to engage in life and business successfully. People will be the #1 asset throughout your life. When you need a job, being able to pick up the phone and make two calls to colleagues who have told you, "If you ever make a career change, call me," is powerful. Or, when you have an employee quit out of nowhere, and you can call three people you know would love to work for your company. Or, your car breaks down and you can make a call to someone who will come to help you. Having a large connection of people within your network of life will make life easier, more resourceful, and more rewarding.

I've learned throughout my entire life that there are a few vital things to remember when you look at the PEOPLE you most closely surround yourself with:

- You never "ARRIVE" and know everything to where you need no one…we all need people.
- You CANNOT do "life" alone.
- You ARE the PEOPLE you surround yourself with.
- Choose them WISELY.

You Never Arrive

Have you ever talked with someone who dominates the conversation? You can't get a word in edgewise, and when you do, even if you prove them wrong, they continue to defend their view? Or, the person who has reached a certain level of success in life, and because of that success, believes they are automatically an expert and other opinions don't really matter? These people think they have arrived, and therefore, other people and their thoughts or opinions aren't needed any longer. They couldn't be further from the truth, though. No matter how successful you are, there is always someone who knows more and something new to be learned. To be successful in life, you need to make sure your circle of people includes people smarter and more talented than you are, for two reasons:

1. You are challenged to excel and keep growing.
2. You have better experts and resources to help you in many areas of life and business, when needed.

No matter how much you know, how successful or fulfilled you become in life, don't fall for the notion you have "arrived in life," to where you "know it all" and don't need anyone. Be open, humble, friendly, and embrace as many people around you as possible. There is always someone to learn something from.

Don't Do Life Alone

So, when you look at your life, do you feel like you are living it alone or there seems to be no one around helping you? Do you feel like you need no one to help you in life?

People are a MUST in life. It's too busy, chaotic, and tough to try and do it alone. To maximize your success and quality of life, you need to continually grow the people who are screaming your name and begging for more in three areas:

People Closest to You

These are people around you who know your heart, soul, and mind. They know everything about you and want to help you succeed. These are people you would go to, ask advice from, and spend lots of quality time with.

People Who Are Acquaintances

These are people who you have a friendship with, colleagues in the business world, or anyone else you see occasionally, but aren't close to.

People Who Know You, but You May Not Know Them

These are people, who somehow have obtained a level of knowledge about you, but you have never personally met them. They could be customers, friends of friends, people who read your blog, etc.

As I stated in chapter three, everyone you meet in life will fall into one of these categories. All of them have an impact on your life at some level, which is why you want to seek to grow in a positive way with each group. Just like you may never know where you will end up, you may never know what person in your life will come out of nowhere to help you in life.

Let me tell you a story about the power of people in life. So, I had shared with you that I founded JaxMetroLive in 2002, and by the summer of 2005, it was very successful at reaching the local community for its cause, but never quite gained enough funding to make it a full-time job for me. I eventually came to a point where I had to look to go back into the corporate world and use my talents there. That was a little scary, given that I had been passed over for eight senior management level jobs just four years earlier. But having a family that I needed to provide for, I made the leap to start looking for my next career. After doing some soul searching, I decided to interview with numerous life insurance and financial planning companies. Insurance and financial planning is where I had my first professional job, so I had some experience. Plus, coming from the non-profit sector of associations, I knew how to speak the language to help non-profit boards provide their executives a nice retirement package; I had also served as CEO of a trade association for seven years prior.

I interviewed with four companies and decided on one. I jumped in with a lot of passion and energy, making my prospect calls to close friends, family, and local non-profits. One of my phone calls was to a local trade association CEO that I met ten years earlier at some association meetings, but then I never saw him after that. We vaguely got to know one another during the meetings ten years earlier. I reached out to him to discuss his financial plan, hoping that he might be able to introduce me to some of his CEO colleagues to help with their financial plans once I had proven myself with his plan. I left a message for him and never thought much about it.

A couple of weeks later I got a call from him. I asked him to go to lunch, which he agreed to. Before I left the call, he asked me what I thought about getting back into the association management field, and I told him that I thought about it on occasion, but gave no serious consideration, given that there weren't many of those types of jobs in my home town. I told him I had some good things moving with some new clients, and thought financial planning was going to be great for my future.

The next week, we met for lunch. We talked about a lot of things, including his plan, what his goals were at retirement, and how much longer he planned to work. As I was talking with him, he kept asking me certain questions about myself and my future. Mentally, I began to think, "It sounds like he is interviewing me to come work for him." After I asked him a few more questions, I couldn't take it any longer. I asked him straight up, "It sounds like you're interviewing me to come work for you. What's up with that?"

He laughed and said, "Tom, I am interviewing you to come work for me." He went on to explain that the number two person in his company did not have the skill set and strengths to lead the association into the future once he retired. When he discovered that, he said he began to think of who he could hire to work for him for two years, to learn everything, then take over as CEO. He knew I lived in Jacksonville, and said to me, "I didn't think I would have to look further than Tom Morrison, so that's why I called you." I asked him why he felt so strongly that I was "the person" to lead their association into the future. He said, "I remember being in the meetings with you ten years ago, and you were the person who always had the bright, fresh ideas and call to action. You were the one with the energy and passion that caught everyone's attention. That's what we need from someone to move our association into the future…someone who can light a fire in our industry. I think that person is you."

Inside I'm thinking, "Wow, this is amazing. I haven't seen him in over eight years and he wants to hire me from the impression that I made over eight years ago." It taught me a valuable lesson…to always leave a good impression with everyone you meet. First impressions are important, but lasting impressions stay with people.

You Are Who You Surround Yourself With

This section is so crucial for you to understand. We are all built for relationships. We want to connect and bond. We want to gain acceptance from our peers and friends. So much so, that we will, in some cases, compromise our principles, what we believe, and even our body, to gain their acceptance.

What I've experienced in life is that the people you hang with on a regular basis will begin to influence your character and the perceptions that other people have of you.

I always tell other professionals when they are out with clients or colleagues that they must be aware of where they are, who they are with, and who could be watching. If you land in the wrong crowd on a regular basis, people will begin to associate you with that crowd, whether good or bad. You may even begin to pick up their bad life habits, whether personal or professional.

Compromising yourself can happen so subtly that you don't even know it right away. I learned this at an early age. It was 1979; I was 15 years old and a sophomore in high school. I had gotten my first job as a lawn maintenance guy at an apartment complex. I worked with my uncle and cousin, and we took great pride in making sure the tenants had the best looking grounds to come home to. One day, a new guy started. He seemed pretty cool and friendly. We had a good time while we worked and got along well. However, I noticed that he would take off for a break ten minutes early, stay later on breaks, and walk the long way back after lunchtime. He would almost waste the entire last half hour of each day doing nothing. He could look busy, but he really wasn't committed to the same level of service to the lawn maintenance area as my cousin and I were. Because we got along, I didn't think anything of it at first. When he left for break, I would go with him. I would stay later than normal on lunch break. The next thing I know, I'm doing the same thing that he is. I was wasting at least an hour a day trying to not work very hard. It only

took one talk from the foreman, my uncle, to get me back
on track to demonstrating excellence in my work ethic,
which I prided myself on. I quickly realized that I was
compromising my work ethic and my reputation, just to
gain a new friend and to feel accepted.

Needless to say, the new guy was let go soon after
because he didn't have the level of work ethic that we
demanded at the company. That could have been me. The
people you hang out with on a regular basis will rub off on
you. You get to decide what kind of character is going to
rub off on you…make good choices.

Choose People Wisely

As my examples in this section show, people you hang
with on a regular basis will have a positive or negative
impact on your life, so CHOOSE THEM WISELY.

The people you surround yourself with don't have to
have the same purpose, passion, principles, or priorities as
you, but they do need to be aligned with your character,
integrity, and goals.

If you want to be an "A" student in school and you are
hanging with "C" students, you will end up being a "C"
student. If drugs aren't your thing, and you hang with
friends who do drugs, you eventually risk compromising
yourself and doing drugs. If you want to have a thriving,
successful business and you hang out with owners who are
continually struggling in business, you will never thrive,

simply survive. If you want to be the top sales person in your company, you don't hang with and learn from those who just want to make the minimum production goals.

If you want to succeed in life and achieve the quality of life that I'm sharing in this book, yet you spend all your time with people who have no life plan, live in daily drama, and blame everyone else for their lot in life, then you will eventually do the same.

When you choose who you hang with on a regular basis, both personally and professionally, make sure to get to know who they are, what they want out of life, what they are committed to, and who *they* hang with. This will give you a good since of their principles, purpose, passion, and priorities, so you can make sure they are headed in the same direction as your life is.

The key is to surround yourself with people who challenge you to grow, who are not afraid to tell you what you need to hear, who ask the hard questions, who are there when you need them, and most importantly, who encourage you on your life journey.

When choosing with whom to surround yourself, you also need to make sure they have good character and integrity. A person of character and integrity is defined as someone whose beliefs and behaviors are in direct alignment with their purpose in life. They say what they mean, and mean what they say.

Choose people who are better than you are. Think

about it...if you want to improve your golf game, you don't ask someone who shoots ten strokes worse than you how to improve. You ask someone who is shooting ten strokes better than you. The same holds true in business and life.

The greatest leaders, business owners, and most successful people in life surround themselves with a team of people who will help them to achieve their goals. When you look at your goals in life, are the people you are surrounding yourself with having a positive or negative impact on you achieving your goals? If they are having a negative impact or holding you back, you need to make a serious change in who you spend your time with. This doesn't mean you alienate the negative people your life. You can still have a bond with them, and you can help to encourage their life to be better, but if you are going to excel in life and reach the goals you want, then you need to expand your network of people who will positively help your life grow every day, and who are moving in the same direction as you are.

Step out of your comfort zone. Look at your PURPOSE, PASSIONS, PRINCIPLES, and PRIORITIES, and start assembling the network of PEOPLE that can help you achieve excellence, excitement, and success.

Do it TODAY and make today the START OF THE REST OF YOUR LIFE!

Application to the Ultimate Life

How do you feel the people in your life help you to be fulfilled in life?

Describe the people you feel are holding you back and what you need to do to correct that?

What would you like to change about the group of people who are in your life the most?

What groups of people could you begin to join, so you will meet others who are headed in the same life direction as you?

Action Steps to the Ultimate Life

Write down three action steps you are going to do in the next 30 days to improve the types of people who are in your life on a regular basis?

1.

2.

3.

Chapter 11
Pushing Past Your Past

"As long as your past is in front of you, you will never achieve the quality of life that you want. You must put your past in the past and never look back."

Let's face it, many people know their PURPOSE and PASSIONS, have their PRIORITIES in order, have solid PRINCIPLES and are surrounded with great PEOPLE, and still never achieve their maximum potential because of one thing: their PAST.

In today's world, there is a lot of hurt and pain in individuals. That pain leads to fear, low self-esteem, lack of confidence, hesitation and unwillingness to take risks. All of these are huge obstacles preventing people from living the ultimate life.

Many people have pain in their life from divorce, abuse, bad relationships with their father, mother, boyfriends, girlfriends, being betrayed by a business partner, or just life experiences. Too many things in your past give subconscious control of your emotions over to those who have hurt you in your life. Because of that hurt, you never move forward and achieve all the potential and excitement you desire in your life.

I can remember my divorce that happened in my early 30's. It happened over her falling in love with another man after six years of marriage. It wasn't meant to happen. It just happened. We were a young couple with two kids and I wasn't seeking to be all I was meant to be, which opened up the door to a great saying I once read on Facebook, "Never give someone the opportunity to make your spouse smile for them."

The funny thing was, I can remember her standing in our bedroom door telling me that I'm worth more than what I'm making. I needed to go out and stake my claim in the world to build a solid future for our family. She would tell me that I was destined to do something really special in life. As with many young men, I listened, and let it go in one ear and out the other, and it opened the door for another man to make her smile.

She wasn't asking me to win the lotto or make the next rich discovery. She just wanted me to grow into the man I was meant to be for our family. I thought I was doing the best I could, but looking back, I wasn't. I was content just making our bills, playing with the kids, and playing husband. By the way, instead of making more money, I was financing our lifestyle on credit cards. To make a long story short without all of the gory details, we ended up divorced and I assumed the mounds of credit card debt that I had allowed us to accumulate. The divorce drove a deep wedge in my soul. I never thought I would be divorced. I was now separated from my kids. It was a bad feeling, and I know many reading this book have been there too.

Within a year of the divorce, she married the man she had fallen in love with and moved our kids with her to Jacksonville. That intensified the pain even more because I adored my children like no other father. I loved being their Dad, and now I couldn't just drive over, pick them up, and take them out to the movies or the park. We had to really live the every other weekend life, meeting halfway between Orlando and Jacksonville to do the exchange.

Over the next two years, I had this internal anger that just sat in a black box in my soul. It never showed its head publically, and you would never know that there was any pain going on inside of me if you were close to me. God was slowly working on me in the healing process, but the internal anger was there. It kept me up at night. It made me second-guess everything I had ever done. It made me think twice about opening my heart up to anyone else ever again.

The bad part about your past is that it will suck the life out of you if you let it. It will haunt you. It will keep you down. It will make you feel like you aren't worth anything.

The good part about your past, and what I learned from my first divorce, is that good can come from your past if you just let it. Your past mistakes are your opportunities to learn how to do things differently in the future and to persevere. Your life doesn't end when bad things happen-that's when life begins. The biggest lessons that I took away from that time in my life are:

- Moving past the past is oftentimes a choice.
- If you are going to be all that you can be, you MUST forgive those who have wronged you.

When I looked at what took place in many other divorces, I saw hate, manipulation, and stress. Two things that I didn't want to teach my children in this process were how to hate and manipulate. I wanted my kids to learn how to excel and love in a time when many feel you should be at your worst.

I began to make a choice to get past my past. I made a choice to not argue with their mom in front of them. I made a choice to not talk bad about her in front of them. I made a choice to treat them with decency when we were all together. I made choices to not let my circumstances control my life. I was determined to rise above them because I KNEW that if I was going to heal sooner, rather than later, and take my life to a new positive level, I had to get the past from out in front of me. So I made a choice.

The second step I mentioned was forgiveness. You know, it really is true, that time has a way of healing wounds. I can remember the day like it was yesterday. It was Easter Sunday and God had been pulling at my heart to do what many never have the strength and nerve to do…forgive my first wife and her husband for their affair. I couldn't help but think that I needed to do it. I had this internal box of anger that wanted to get out, even though I wouldn't let it control my life, but it was still there. I remember dropping my kids off to them after Easter service and then driving away. As I drove away, my heart was pulling me back to return and forgive, in person, for all that happened in the past. I wanted to make a choice to pull out the black box of anger in my soul and throw it away. I wanted to be free of the anger, and I didn't want it controlling even 1% of my life. So I turned around, asked them to meet me in the driveway of the house and talk. They had no idea what I wanted to say. I proceeded to thank them for being awesome parents to our children; we all know what hangs over us from the past, and I didn't want those circumstances to rule our lives any longer. I wanted to cast out all the guilt, shame, anger, and negativity in our lives that were associated with the past. I told them that I loved them both and I forgave them for everything that took place in our life. I hugged them both and left to celebrate Easter Sunday.

FREEDOM! FREEDOM! FREEDOM! You can't believe the weight off my chest that day. I could move on with life 100% without any thought of the past holding me back in life. That moment empowered me to be all I could be. It strengthened my soul to allow my life to climb to new levels, emotionally and relationally.

Today, my children's mother and her husband and I are great friends, living a life free of hate and full of love and joy. More importantly, our kids didn't learn how to hate, they learned how to love. They learned how to make a choice to forgive.

So what's in your past? What is holding you back? Who do you need to reach out to and have a discussion with, to say things you have always wanted to say?

You need to eliminate the negativity of your past. You need to eliminate time-wasters from your life. You need to know you were put here for a PURPOSE and to affect PEOPLE in positive ways. Don't let your past and negative people drown your dreams. Eliminate them and pursue your dreams with all your might.

As I conclude this chapter, there is a third lesson that I learned beyond making a choice to let the past go and forgive. It was to find someone, or a group of people, that will allow you to "empty the bucket" on them. When life deals you a significant blow, all of these emotions and thoughts start filling up your brain and your soul. It's like a balloon filling up with air. If you don't let some of the air out at some point, that baby is going to explode! The last thing you need to do is to explode in the wrong place. Find someone, or a small group of people, who know your circumstances, know who you are at your core, and have your best interest at heart. Meet with them periodically to just share what you're thinking. Get it out…get the anger out…get the hate out. Once it's all out, talk about what you need to do to recover and move forward.

For some, you may need a professional counselor to work through your issues. Don't be ashamed to see a counselor, they are professionals at helping people to move from pain to pleasure…from hate to love…and addiction to recovery. Find one, and start healing today.

In order for you to experience a life of freedom and to maximize your potential, you must let your past go. You must turn from looking back, so you can put focus on the future. When it comes to experiencing the fun, excitement, opportunities, and freedom that life has to offer, your past is like a huge bag of rocks weighing you down.

Letting your past go means dealing with your unfinished business. Unfinished business means facing your past. This means having the discussion with whomever was involved to reconcile the issue, and most importantly, FORGIVING whoever wronged you.

Forgiveness is the most important part of this process. Remember, forgiveness is not about letting someone off the hook; it's about un-strapping the bag of rocks on your back with all the pain, and letting it go. Let your past be a set of lessons for a brighter future, not a set of obstacles that break you down and keep you from your future. To forgive, you don't even have to talk to the person, you can simply write them a letter, an email, or just in your mind have that conversation with yourself, and forgive the other person.

From there...you walk forward in FREEDOM, with a renewed feeling of joy, excitement, and optimism.

If you have a desire to experience the ultimate life, do whatever it takes to wipe away the pain of the past. Let today start the rest of YOUR LIFE. Your future awaits you!

Application to the Ultimate Life

What is in your past that you feel is holding you back from experiencing all that life has to offer?
Who do you feel has wronged you in a way that is holding you back from being all you can be in life?
What would you want to say to each of these people?

Action Steps to the Ultimate Life
What choices do you need to make, starting today, to help

you let go of your past?

Who are you going to forgive this week, so you can be free from your past?

Who are you going to ask to let you "empty the bucket" every now and then to get the negative things off your chest and make positive steps in your life?

Chapter 12
Planning Your Path

"You need to live out your life with an end game in mind. If you don't know where you want to go, you will never be able to plan how to get there."

One of the most important parts of my list of "P's" is PLANNING your PATH. Planning is very important in life because it provides you with a clear path toward the pursuit of your goals. People have confidence in people who plan. It lets them know that you aren't just guessing about how to accomplish your purpose. It says that you are serious about moving forward, and you aren't just winging it. People want to follow someone with a plan. If you want people to scream your name and beg for more in your life, it's important that you have a plan for your life.

As I said in chapter two, it doesn't matter where you are in life...poor, unemployed, in a job you hate, in a bad marriage, parenting a rebellious child, working for a horrible boss, or happy and just wanting to move to a better place in life, you are only one decision and three action steps away from transforming your life from where you are to where you want to be.

LET ME SAY THAT AGAIN...YOU ARE ONLY ONE DECISION AND THREE ACTION STEPS AWAY FROM TRANSFORMING YOUR LIFE FROM WHERE YOU ARE TO WHERE YOU WANT TO BE.

If you are in circumstances that you do not like, or want to move to another level, all you need to do is the following:

- Write down where you want to be in three to five years from now.
- Write down three things that you need to do within the next 12 months to make that happen.
- Write down three things that you need to do within the next 90 days to make that happen.

Once you decide where you want to go, have written down the three actions steps to take within a year, and the three action steps to take within the next 90 days, all you need to do is GO…TAKE ACTION. Once you decide to go, you take the first three action steps that you have written down in your plan. Every time you complete three action steps, write three more down. Success is always being able to do the next three action steps successfully. Before you know it, five years have passed and you have accomplished your big goal just by acting on all the small steps that you needed to get there.

When you begin to think through your life plan, there are four areas that you need to have a plan for and put thought into:

Relationship Development

Relationships are everywhere in your life. It's what this entire book is about. People will build you up or tear you down. Have a plan to develop your relationships so they may be a building agent in your life.

Spiritual Growth

For many people like me, some level of spiritual growth is vastly important. It gives them a sense of self-worth and overall purpose knowing that there is something larger than their life here on earth. Spiritual growth plays a huge role in keeping you disciplined in your life and living in a way that lets you be a positive impact on other people's lives. Beyond that, one feels great confidence in life, knowing that when you come to the end of yourself and have no more energy to give to your goals or passions, there is a greater source to call upon who makes things happen beyond you.

Physical Health

I've learned in life that you should never make decisions when you are tired or not feeling well. A big part of being physically fit is making sure that you get enough rest, eat right, and have a continuous routine of physical activity that provides the energy you need to be successful, day in and day out. I will address this in a later chapter.

Financial Accumulation

I remember giving my son a birthday card that read, "Money isn't everything, but it sure makes life easier." Financial pressures cause great stress in life, and they are the number one reason that many marriages struggle today. Financial insecurity plays a huge role in the emotions of a family. When things are tight, attitudes are tight. It is important that you have a plan of financial growth to relieve those pressures. I'm going to talk about this as well, in a later chapter.

Life planning doesn't have to be complicated or long-range. So many people spend so much time doing a comprehensive five and ten year plan, and the events that impact their plan are going to change dramatically in the next three years. With technology, the economy, and many other elements changing at such a rapid pace, things change way too fast to think in terms of five and ten year plans, in my opinion. Think in short term increments to obtain a long-term dream or goal. I will talk later on how to put an effective life plan together, and how often to review it.

A plan allows you to work through each facet that can impact you and prepare for it so that you stay on a clear path to your goals. Life comes at us fast and it is easy to veer off course. The next thing you know, what was going to take you two years to accomplish is now going to take you four years because you got off-track and made a bad choice.

Imagine if you were in Miami, Florida, and you were given the goal of being in Seattle, Washington, in seven days. That is a 3,300 mile journey. At 500 miles a day, that would take you almost seven days. If you left Miami without a map in hand or a GPS, you would never make it there in seven days. You wouldn't know in what direction to go, and any obstacles that may come up would delay your trip. By planning and looking at the proper resources ahead of time, you are able to determine the quickest path to your destination without the headache of being lost or delayed. You can pre-think any unforeseen obstacles that might delay your trip like weather, traffic, potential accidents and even plan an alternate route to get around the delay. However a map or a GPS device is your best resource to help you get there on time.

Life and business are the same way. In order to accomplish your goals, it is important that you work through a plan that sets your path clearly in the direction of your goals. It is important that you sit down and think about your goals on a consistent basis, and brainstorm the things that might delay your plans so you can come up with solutions to the "what if this happens" scenarios. The key in the "what if this happens" review is to focus on the things you can control. So many people get caught up in worrying over the things that they can't control, and they forget that they actually have numerous actions that they can take to influence their path in life and keep it moving forward.

When adversity happens that disrupt people's lives, it makes me think of the old saying, "People can't see the forest for the trees." What people fail to do in this mindset is simply look down and realize there is a chainsaw right beside them to cut the trees down the bad trees to see the forest." Sometimes it pays to look around in the midst of adversity. The solutions to the obstacles blocking your path are typically right near you.

This doesn't mean that you ignore all the things that you can't control. You do take the time to work through them and write down a contingency plan in the event that it actually happens, but you don't let it take the focus away from the action steps that you can actually take.

Another key part of planning is, "Quit planning for a future that you cannot predict, and start planning for the future that you WANT!" It's a totally different mindset when you pursue what you want. Most people wander around, lost in disbelief, because they can't predict the future and forget that they actually have control over many things that can help them to achieve their purpose and goals.

The key to any plan is to have it written down somewhere. If it's written down, you remember it and you can be held accountable for it. A plan without accountability is no plan at all. When you are writing your plan down, you want to make sure that you have a stated set of goals at the top. From there, you write down the action steps that you need to take in order to achieve your goals in the next 12 months and the next 90 days. Beside each action step you should have what you need to accomplish, a date to accomplish it by, and any people listed who can help you succeed in that action step.

Your success in your life plan will depend on the Pillars and Characteristics that I outlined in my **Path to the Ultimate Life** visual. How you respond to challenges along the way will also determine your rate of success. Never see challenges as an end to your dreams and goals. Challenges are opportunities to learn and grow from, with perseverance. Never give up. Never quit. If things don't seem to be going right, you may need to make changes in your plan in order to achieve your goals.

As you are living out your life plan, it's important that you review it at periodic points so that you can make sure you are on the right course. I always suggest looking at a life plan every three to four months. With things changing so fast in the world, you must be able to adjust your plan as the environment around you changes. Your review should be as easy as asking the following questions:

- Where should I be in pursuing my goal?
- Where am I?
- What should I be doing differently?
- What am I not doing that I should be doing?
- What should I stop doing because it's done or because it's a waste of my time?
- What is my plan of attack to make up the difference, if there is a gap between where I should be and where I am.

The problem with any planning in life is that many do not write their actual plans down…leaving them to wing it. A year later, they are wondering why they are still in the same place, spinning their wheels. The key in making a plan become your reality is to write it down, act on it, review it, adjust it, if needed, and repeat the process.

Your plan should be specific enough to keep you on

course towards your purpose, but agile and flexible enough to take on new opportunities that may allow you to reach your purpose more quickly, or in a way you never thought possible.

As you work on your life plan, there are two areas you want to make sure you think through carefully:

Identify the Threats to Achieving Your Purpose & Goals

On your journey towards achieving your purpose, various obstacles are going to get in the way. They may be the economy, an ineffective boss, divorce, or a competitor. Regardless of what they are, you need to identify what those threats are and then determine whether they are controllable or uncontrollable. If they are uncontrollable, write down what you should do as a contingency, if it were to occur. If it is controllable, this is where you want to put your real effort. I have found in my life that most people are so worried about what they can't control, that they forget to be 100% effective and focused on what they can control. Have the action steps that you may need to take for the uncontrollable things in your life, but focus 100% of your effort on all of the things that you DO HAVE CONTROL OF on your path to success.

Identify the Resources and People That You Have at Your Disposal to Achieve Your Purpose and Goals

These are the tools and network that you will use to overcome the obstacles in step 1, and to take advantage of the opportunities that come your way. Resources may be your job, your network of people, or training that you are involved in. After you have a full list of resources, brainstorm what resources you need to acquire to be more effective at achieving your purpose and goals for life. Once you have this full list, you will have all the tools that you need to be successful.

I want to end this chapter on the "financial accumulation" issue because it is a biggie. It is so important for you to have a financial plan in the areas of meeting monthly expenses, liquidity for unforeseen expenses, and retirement planning.

Ever since I was 20 years old, I have had an excel spreadsheet budget. It has helped me to look at the reality of what I can and cannot afford. So many people live above their means because they don't know that they don't have enough money to pay their bills. They keep racking up debt with credit cards and credit lines to live a lifestyle that they can't afford. Planning your monthly financial budget is easy. Whether you write them down or use an excel spreadsheet, do the following:

- Make twelve columns, one for each month.
- Put a total column at the end for the year.

- Write all sources of income on the first line for each month.
- Write your monthly expenses for each month.
- Add each column up at the bottom.

You will quickly see what months you have extra income or a deficit, and how much money you should have at the end of the year. This is usually an eye opener for most people because it shows them that they don't have much money to spend after bills. This is the number one reason that people don't do budgeting, because they don't want to see the reality of what they can't spend money on. Instead, they just keep spending and racking up debt. They want to keep "robbing Peter to pay Paul." Don't let yourself get in this rut. Do an annual budget to see where you lack, and start planning on how you can enhance your income to achieve your financial goals. Remember, in my opinion, financial pressures are the number one reason for stress in many marriages and businesses. Make a plan so you minimize those pressures.

When it comes to financial liquidity for the unexpected, it is crucial that you have one or both of the following items: money in savings and/or a credit card that you can access to pay for big expenditures. This must be with the intent that you will pay it off in a short period of time…like three to four months. Always have a way to pay for a $500 to $2,000 unexpected event…they are going to happen…that's life.

When it comes to retirement, many people think the illustrious notion of retirement "just happens." They spend their entire life having fun and then wake up at sixty with the reality that they don't have enough saved to quit working. What you need to know, though, is that one of the greatest things ever created is compound interest. Compound interest is interest that continues to accumulate on top of itself, over time, with your investments. Over a span of twenty years, it will amount to more money than you would have thought when you first started investing on day one.

I wasn't taught this at a young age, and didn't start thinking about retirement savings until I was 48. The amount that I am having to put away, to one day fully retire and enjoy life, is seven times the amount of money that my children would have to put away if they start at age 25. If you don't start early, the amount of money you have to put away each month can almost be too much.

I can remember when the IRA deduction was $1,000 a year in my 20's. I can remember saying to myself, that won't amount to anything over time. When you do the math, it really does add up. While writing this book, I did a little study of my life earnings. I wondered what would have been the impact of my life savings had I learned to live without just five percent of my annual wages and invested them in a set of highly rated mutual funds that follow the S & P 500. Most experts will tell you that over the long term, you will get somewhere around twelve percent a year on average, investing over twenty plus years. I discounted the rate of return to ten percent, just to be conservative. Knowing this, I did a spreadsheet, taking ten percent of my earnings since age twenty-two and adding interest to that annual savings each year to see what my life savings for retirement would be at 65. I was surprised that my pot of money to retire with was over $1,200,000. Yes, I said, one point two million dollars.

Failing to do this type of planning will leave you somewhat desperate near retirement because you will be left with whatever social security is going to look like when you reach retirement age. Don't get caught at any age thinking retirement just happens. It doesn't. Plan, and plan early, even if it is just putting away $100 a month into an IRA. To see the reality of this visually, I want you to take a close look at the following visual that I created when I was in financial planning. It represents the four stages of life:

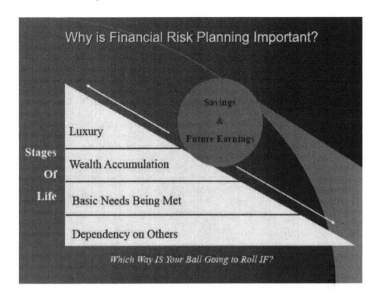

Stage one is childhood through college. From birth to college, almost everyone is dependent on parents, grandparents, family, and friends.

Stage two is mid 20's and early marriage. During our 20's and early 30's, many get married, have children, and pretty much meet their basic needs. It can be tough to save much on your own, given the expense of a home and children. This is a good stage in which to try and land a job with a good company with some type of matched retirement plan.

Stage three is your mid 30's though retirement. 35 to 60 are traditionally a person's highest, and prime earning years and where wealth accumulation happens. Expenses should begin to lower in your late 50's with children graduating college and no longer dependent on you for financial needs.

Stage four is supposed to be actual retirement. You spend your entire life pushing the ball of savings up the hill, hoping to get to the final stage and retire.

The real data from a study done in 2000 by the Social Security Office of Research and Statistics, tells us that of all adults who reach 25 years of age, 16% will pass on before age 65, 18% will be financially independent, and 66% will have their "ball" roll all the way back down the hill by age 65, depending on others for one or more of the following: housing, healthcare, transportation, and food. 66%!

If you look at the average net worth of people age 65, as reported by CNN Money in 2014, it is $232,000. That may sound like a lot of money to some people…especially young people. Here is the reality: if you have $232,000 in savings, and you are taking out the suggested 4% a year by financial planning experts so you don't run out of money too quickly, you will be living on an annual income of $9,280. If you add an estimated $20,000 from Social Security, that's only $29,280 a year. You can't pay for housing, transportation, health care and food on $2,440 a month. It's no wonder 66% of people reaching age 65 are reliant on others to live out the rest of their life.

If you are one of those 66%, that means relying on your kids, family, and maybe friends for health care, living expenses, housing, etc. If they aren't there for you, who will take care of you and where will you live? Nursing homes are filled with parents whose children never come see them. Will this be you?

I want to highly, highly encourage everyone reading this book to take the time to sit down NOW, and access your financial risk plan. Things that cause the ball to roll backwards include divorce, a daughter's wedding (or weddings if you have more than one daughter), unexpected disability/death, taxes, job change, being fired/down-sized, etc. These are all "threats" to your idea of retirement in the future and a good quality of life. The earlier you put a plan in place, the less expensive it is to cover the risk and do something about it. If you want to have a $60,000 a year income at 65, and Social Security pays you $20,000 a year, you need at least $1,000,000 in the bank just to take out the 4% suggested by financial planning experts. Are you on target to have a million in savings at age 65? If not, it's time to get serious about your plan...NOW. The biggest threat to your plan is choosing NOT TO PLAN.

I'm sure by now many of you are asking yourself, why I did not include "professional career planning" in the planning process. Career planning is not one of the key pillars of life. Career planning is a part of your financial plan, and is a subset of the decisions you make on what type of lifestyle you want, and how you want to live. Many people go into business for themselves because they want the freedom to own their time and to do the things that they enjoy when they want to…not when they get a week of vacation from a boss. Others like working for someone else. Depending on how you want to spend your time and money will dictate the direction of the professional career you need to pursue.

As you are looking at the four areas I have shared, take a look at your professional career or business and ask yourself, "Is it helping build my four key areas of life, or is it taking away from my four key areas discussed at the beginning of this chapter?" If it's not building, and you are not happy, you may want to look at making a change. Don't let your career drive who you are or how you live your life. Let your life and who you are drive your career. Your heart and soul will love you for it.

Before you leave this chapter, stare at the four stages of life graph that I shared earlier:

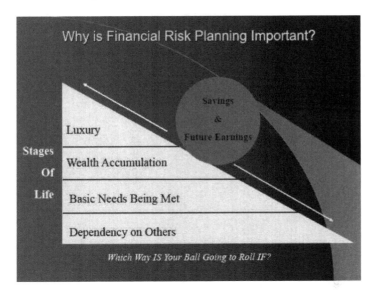

Why is Financial Risk Planning Important?

Stages Of Life

Luxury

Savings & Future Earnings

Wealth Accumulation

Basic Needs Being Met

Dependency on Others

Which Way IS Your Ball Going to Roll IF?

Where are you on the graph? Is the reality that you will be relying on others after age 65? Don't let another day go by without putting some thought into where you are, where you want to be, and a plan to make up the gap if one exists. Look at each area of relationships, spiritual, physical, and financial. When you are in the second half of your life, you will be very happy you did.

Application to the Ultimate Life

What do you need to improve in your relationships to reach the quality of life you want?

What areas of your spiritual life do you need to be better at? Does your spiritual belief align with your behaviors?

What do you need to do differently in your physical life to

be able to stay healthy for your family, employees, and friends?

On a scale from 1 to 10, with 10 being on target, and 1 not being on target, rate yourself on the following:

_____   Meeting your monthly expenses without credit card debt

_____   Having the means to pay for an unexpected bill

_____   Being on target at your current age to retire at age 65

What do you have to do in order to be better at managing your finances?

What are you willing to sacrifice to help you save the money for your future?

Action Steps to the Ultimate Life

Where do you want to be in three years in the following areas:

Relationships:

Spiritually:

Physically:

Financially:

Write down your three action steps that you need to make in the next 90 days and in 12 months in the following areas, to put you on track to reach your goals:

90 Day Action Steps

1.

2.

3.

12 Month Action Steps

1.

2.

3.

Chapter 13
Pause and Meditation

"It's in the moment of pause that you confirm you are headed in the right direction or that you need to shift to another direction."

So let's look at where you are at this point in the book. You have worked on Defining your PURPOSE, Discovering your PASSION, Deciding on PRINCIPLES, Setting your PRIORITIES, Looking at the PEOPLE you need to surround yourself with, and Working through your PAST. Now you have a solid PLAN to obtain the ultimate life. You are ready to go! But wait...there is a moment when we have to pause and think about our plan and path.

Pausing for a moment is so crucial because some of us can be selfish about what we want in life. Some people are impulsive in how they pursue life, and some people have made a series of bad choices in the past. It is a healthy thing, after all of these steps, to pause and just let all of your plans settle a bit.

People love to be associated with people who take time to pause and meditate on things that are meaningful. It gives them confidence that you won't be running into something without thinking about it. Do people like people who are pioneers? Of course they do. I'm a huge pioneer in life, but I have learned when to be a pioneer, and when to pause and meditate before acting. The bigger the risk, the more reason one must pause and meditate. If you want people to scream your name and beg for more, you need to learn when to be a pioneer, and when to pause and meditate on a plan before pursuing it. Even take the time to share your plan with someone that you trust to look at it and give you sound feedback.

Anytime you work through your life plan, at any level, it is going to create big change. It is a good step to take a few days and sit on the ideas, discuss them with your closest friends/mentors, and make sure that you have thought of everything. Now, not every decision needs this kind of pause, but many should, especially if you feel that your decisions have caused you to veer off course in your life. You need someone who has a history of making good decisions that created success to help you talk through what you are about to do.

My life has benefited tremendously from the close friendships that I have had. They are people who know my heart, know how I think, and know my dreams and desires. At any given time, I could get on the phone or meet them in person and discuss any major decision in my life or business and receive invaluable feedback.

I've already told the story of the friend who encouraged me to start my singles ministry. He knew my heart and passion to make a difference in single adults, who were struggling in the world of relationships. I was getting ready to gear up a plan to look at other jobs when, in my moment of pause, he encouraged me to think about another route. Out of that pause came an organization that over three years, reached over 10,000 single adults, from over 150 churches. Many shared their stories about how JaxMetroLive played a major role in them finding their purpose in life, walking away from drugs…the bar scene, and getting their life on the right track. I'm so glad I chose to pause and talk about my plan with my friend.

I can remember another time, well into my singles ministry, when it wasn't bringing in enough money to fully support me as a full-time staff person. I was holding out for it to happen and allowing my family to suffer financially. I got caught up in the moment, with wanting to do my passion full-time. It wasn't happening fast enough, but because I was so emotionally invested, I kept pounding the pavement for the funding to create the success that it needed in order to support a full-time staff position. I didn't realize at first the impact that it was having on my marriage and our family unit. Over time, it became very clear.

So I came up with this new plan for funding the ministry, and called one of my closest friends to talk about it. He was very successful...well thought-out, and knew me long before the ministry took off. The call to him was my way of pausing to see if I had the right things in order. The conversation didn't go the way I wanted it to. He proceeded to have a hard conversation with me. He knew my wife and I as a couple, and could see the difficulty that my staying in the ministry was putting on our family. He proceeded to have a hard conversation with me saying, "Tom, your family needs you to use your talents in other ways to make sure the mortgage is paid and there is food on the table. You need to go out this week and find a job so you can work while the ministry gains enough funding to make it full-time." He went on to discuss with me that my wife would see that as an action on my part...that I was willing to do "whatever it takes" to make sure my family had a home, food, and that we could cover our bills. I was like...WHOA! This is not the conversation that I was looking to have. The ministry had been changing hundreds of people's lives every week and I didn't want to leave that full-time. I wanted to stay in it, and I had a plan to make it happen. But in my moment of "pause and meditation," my friend spoke the truth into my life that I needed to hear.

I was ready to dive in and work to create more funding, but what I really needed to do was to go get a job. Within the next week, I met with the coach of my kid's flag football team. He was one of the partners in a nationally growing sub shop. I discussed with him the management opportunities within their company. He saw that I had the type of qualities that they were looking for in their store management teams, and hired me within the week. Over the course of the next year, I saw a change in my relationship with my wife, in that she saw a husband who was willing to do whatever it took to make sure that our family had enough money to make our bills and take the financial pressure off.

This wouldn't have happened had I not taken the time to pause and meditate on my plan and discuss it with someone close to me. Had I gone ahead with my plan, I would have created more pressure in my family than was already there.

Remember, pausing and meditating on your plan isn't only to confirm that you have everything needed for your plan to be successful. Pausing and meditating on your plan is also to determine if you should even follow through with your plan.

Sometimes in your moment of pause and meditation,

when you seek outside counsel from people, you may not hear what you want to hear. Be cautious to NOT turn away their comments simply because they didn't tell you what you wanted to hear. Be open and listen to what they are saying, because when you are so emotionally invested in your decision, you may not be seeing things clearly. I'm a big believer that if you ask three of your mentors/friends about your plan, and you fully explain it to them, and they all tell you it's not a good course of action, then it's probably a plan that you need to seriously rethink.

The big key for pausing and meditating on your life or business plans is to surround yourself with a network of at least three to four mentors, who are willing to listen to you and have honest conversations about your plan. Remember what I talked about in the chapter on people? You want to make sure the people you are surrounding yourself with are the ones headed in the same successful direction as you are.

Application to the Ultimate Life

What is your biggest challenge with pausing and meditating on big decisions in your life?

What is your biggest challenge when talking about your plans or decisions with key mentors or friends before you act?

How does it make you feel when you hear someone say, "I don't think making that decision is in your best interest?"

When you look at the key decisions in your life that you rushed into, how did those decisions turn out? Were there friends telling you not to make that choice? Why didn't you listen?

Action Steps to the Ultimate Life

What decisions do you have coming up that you feel you need to pause and meditate on?

Who are three people you can call for personal and/or business feedback on decisions that you want another opinion on?

Chapter 14
Let's Get Physical

"The decisions that you make in the first half of your life regarding your health will determine how you get to live out the second half of your life...Take it serious."

I know what you are thinking...OMG, Tom is about to tell me I'm out of shape and I need to work out, diet, and step on the scale every Friday morning. Well, I'm not going to do that...well, maybe just a little.

Listen up. I'm here to tell you from personal experience that you need to take a serious look in the mirror and ask yourself, "What are you doing to keep yourself healthy and in good physical shape?" It doesn't matter what age you are, you still need to have a weekly plan for physical activity. It needs to include some level of cardio (to keep your heart healthy and strong), strength training (to keep your body healthy and strong), and it doesn't have to be one or two hours in the gym. It can be swimming, biking, running, as well as high-intensity strength training sets in your own living room...and it only has to last for 30 minutes at a time. Everyone's got 30 minutes of time for their health.

If you want people to scream your name and beg for more, then you need to be where the people are. You need to be able to do things outside your comfort zone. You want to be able to have the energy to put forth the effort to help a friend move, work a few extra hours on an important project, or just do something athletic with your friends, kids, or grandkids.

If you are young, let me help you to understand the "why" in all of this physical health stuff. If you are under thirty and you are over your height verses weight limit or have any type of adverse health conditions, then you need to think seriously about having a weekly plan that includes a healthy diet and at least 30 minutes of working out, at least five times a week. As I said above, all it takes is 30 minutes a day. If you don't take your health (and weight) seriously, then once you hit your forties and fifties, you will pay the price.

If you are young and slim, let me wake you up a bit. I have been an athlete my entire life. I played baseball in middle school, high school, and college. I ran cross-country in college. I ran in my twenties and have pretty much worked out off-and-on my entire life. I also engaged in intramural sports like golf, ultimate frisbee, and basketball in my 30's and 40's. I haven't played as much in my forties and fifties as I once did, but I have always worked out. When I graduated high school, I weighed 135 pounds and had a 29" waist. I was slim, strong, and could run like a deer...forever. When I hit my late 20's, I was 160 pounds and had a 32" waist. I thickened up and filled out, and it actually looked good on me. I was growing into manhood, but by the time I hit my late 30's, I hit 190 pounds and had a 34" waist. BOOM! When I hit 45, I had a 38" waist at 210 pounds...AND I AM A HIGHLY ACTIVE GUY!

Since 45, I have eaten healthy and consistently worked out...just to maintain my waistline, weight, and health. I tell you this as young people to let you know, if you let your body go, it's going to really go in your late 30's and 40's, and will be hard to get back in your 50's- especially, if you have built-in fun habits like eating the wrong thing and drinking socially. Build good habits while you are young. That doesn't mean you can't have fun, but enjoy everything in moderation. Build good habits into your life with a consistent workout and healthy eating. Your body will love you for it, you will feel better every day, and you will give yourself a chance to live a longer life, where you can enjoy each day physically.

Now, let me talk to the people over 30. It's not too late to make a choice to take your health back. The combination of what you put into your body and the lack of physical activity are doing more harm than you can even imagine. At the end of this chapter, I'm going to give you some "do's" and "don'ts" for your life, to help you be committed to being physically healthy.

As I approached 50, I happened to attend a conference in Atlanta, Georgia. Many people reading this book have been to conferences and know what I'm talking about with regards to all-you-can-eat events during the day and hospitality at night. After returning from the conference in Atlanta, I did a lot of self-analyzing about what I experienced with regards to calorie consumption for the days that I was at the conference. Atlanta and its sponsors rolled out the red carpet for the attendees, as any city does for a big conference, and attendees greatly appreciated it…especially me. I love to eat, and love a social drink. As I looked at what we were all putting into our bodies over the four-day period, I began to really take a hard look at what many people put into their bodies on a daily basis. Being married to a personal fitness trainer put it right in my face. We began to discuss the fact that reports show that two-thirds of the American adult population is overweight

and have very poor eating and workout habits. My
questions for you at this point are:

- Do you want to be physically prepared to make the best
  decisions in your life and business?
- Do you want to be physically able to enjoy the fun
  outdoor activities that life offers?
- Do you want to be around when your grandkids are
  born?
- Do you want to see your grandkids grow up and enjoy
  playing with them?
- Do you want to enjoy the last ten years of your life
  without physical ailments?

If the answers to these questions are YES, then you
need to pay attention to this chapter and build the good
habits that will allow you to live out those four questions
above. Studies show that upwards of 80% of health care
costs come from behavior and lifestyle choices that people
make. These choices include, but are not limited to, poor
diet, lack of exercise, smoking, lack of sleep, and/or
excessive drinking. These behaviors can lead to obesity,
high blood pressure, diabetes, stroke, heart attack, and
metabolic syndrome, just to name a few. Now, I'm not
trying to throw fear around lightly, but rather, be real about
the consequences of your daily habits and choices, with
regards to the serious over consumption of calories and

lack of physical activity in today's lifestyle. We love to drink it up. We love our fast food. We love our greasy fried foods...our highly-processed foods…our sugary yummies, and we love our soft drinks. We love. We love. We love!!! You should love to live a LONG LIFE.

Now let me dial it back here for a second. I'm not advocating that you give up everything I just talked about; there is absolutely nothing wrong with having a happy hour. There is nothing wrong with eating fried foods. There is nothing wrong with having fast food. There is nothing wrong with enjoying a sweet treat. BUT, it should all be in moderation. Before I met my wife, I was eating fast food at least three times, sometimes four times a week. That probably wasn't good for my health. Fast food is very tasty, but not overly nutritious, and should be consumed in moderation.

I personally live a very active and fun life in my 50's. I love networking, being out at social events, and doing physically challenging things in work and life, especially with my wife and kids. Life is meant to be lived, right? Well I do! I come at life with a lot of energy, do a lot of crazy stuff that many say they can't do, and typically will dance until late into the night with my wife and friends.

Many ask, "Tom, how do you do it?" Well, in my early 30's, I didn't need to have a plan because the calories just fell off my body, and weight just stayed away. In my late 40's, those same calories began to hang on for dear life, and

the weight was like a magnet to my body. I knew that if I
kept eating like crazy, with no plan for a healthy life style
in my 40's and 50's, I was sure to drive my health into the
ground. Deteriorating health plays a huge role in your
ability to enjoy your life as you grow older. The decisions
that you make for your body before thirty years of age will
have a big impact on how your physical health will be in
your forties and fifties.

When my kids and friends want to go dancing,
kayaking, mountain biking, zip-lining, skiing, white water
rafting or any other physical activity, I don't want my body
to say "no" because of physical limitations. I came to the
conclusion that I needed to build good diet and workout
habits with each decade, to ensure I will be able to keep
enjoying the things I love to do, well into retirement. It all
starts with good health habits in your 20's and 30's, and
redefining those habits in your 40's and 50's.

With the help of my wife, a Personal Trainer and
Health and Wellness Coach, I've developed a balance of
disciplined eating, moderation, and fitness that keep my
body feeling young, energetic, and fit. Three things I've
learned about keeping your body at a weight where you feel
good and remain healthy are:

1. 80% of weight/fat loss (or weight/fat gain) comes
   from the kitchen (what you eat).
2. You can NEVER work out more than the calories

you consume…there's just not enough hours in a day.

3. To get to the weight, and have the toned body you desire, you MUST do both: disciplined eating AND fitness.

For those of you who say, "Tom, I travel too much or don't have the time," your excuses can disappear. There are workouts now that you can do right in your living room or hotel room, using your own body weight and a couple of dumbbells. If you travel, you can structure a highly effective workout to do in your hotel room. If you are busy, you can take 30 minutes of your time, instead of watching a nightly television show. The question is, do you want it bad enough? Are you tired of feeling tired? Are you tired of not fitting into the clothes you would love to wear? Are you tired of not being able to do the things that you want to do because you are not physically able to do them?

I'm encouraging you, whether you are a 20-year old, or a 50-year old, get serious about your health. It's a small investment each day, and the benefits are huge. You will feel better, move better, and look better. You will be more confident in life and work. Your relationships will flourish because your spouse or significant other will see how important it is for you to be in good health for them.

I want you to walk away with some applicable takeaways that will transform your life, so I've put together a list of "10 do's" and "10 don'ts" to help you be more proactive in managing your health. These 20 small action steps will help you work towards a healthier and longer-lasting life, so people will want to scream your name and beg for more. These tips come from my wife, DeAnna, a certified Personal Trainer and Corporate Health Coach:

10 Things You SHOULD Do Weekly

1. Eat...don't skip meals, BUT choose wisely (think veggies and lean proteins at every meal).
2. Pack your own healthy snacks to carry in your bag. This will help you to avoid making bad choices because of low blood sugar.
3. Choose veggies and fruit over other less healthy choices like bread, pasta, and dessert.
4. Eat dessert, BUT only have a bite or two.
5. Drink like a fish...WATER.
6. When drinking mixed drinks, let the mixer be water.
7. Take your vitamins because most of us don't eat enough healthy, whole foods to meet the RDA on many important vitamins and minerals.
8. Try to get 8 hours of sleep.
9. Make time to sweat...every day (even 15-20 minutes of exercise is better than nothing).
10. Have a glass of water in between each "adult" beverage.

10 Things You Should NOT Be Doing Weekly

1. Avoid the high calories/high-carb breakfast goodies (bagels, doughnuts, pastries).
2. Say "No" to the bread and butter on the table.
3. Skip the high calorie/high fat snacks.
4. Don't do soda…not even diet.
5. Avoid the temptations at the office (candy, cookies, and other junk food).
6. Don't do "seconds"…only one pass through the buffet.
7. Say "No" to the floating appetizer trays at parties and events (or, only have one).
8. Avoid the sweet, "fluffy" mixed drinks (there can be as many as several hundred calories in EACH drink).
9. Don't sit for long periods of time (you burn more calories standing and walking).
10. Don't go out with the attitude that you'll eat, drink, and be merry with reckless abandon…it WILL be waiting for you when you get home and step on the scale.

...and remember, along with these 20 shifts in thinking, find a good mobile workout program that you can do anytime, anywhere. Technology is making health and fitness a piece of cake. WAIT, DID I JUST SAY A PIECE OF CAKE? NOT IN THIS CHAPTER…

With a disciplined diet, moderation, and a sound fitness program, you can maintain a healthy lifestyle that will keep your waistline slim, keep health care costs down, and maximize the enjoyment of a long life.

Make a personal commitment to change your habits for your spouse, kids, family, friends, and co-workers who depend on you. Years down the road, you will say it was the best decision that you ever made and you'll be adding years to your life and life to your years.

Application to the Ultimate Life

What don't you like about yourself physically?
What are your challenges with eating a healthy diet on a regular basis?
Why don't you workout? If you do, how can you ensure that you stay disciplined?
What could you change about your schedule that would make time for 30 minutes each day to do some cardio and strength training?
Write down the people in your life for whom it's worth the effort to start a strategy for healthy living.

Action Steps to the Ultimate Life

What is your physical goal in the next 12 months to get yourself in better shape?
How are you going to change your eating habits in the next week to build good habits with your diet?

Chapter 15
Preparation and Practice Are Everything

"In life, preparation without practice will minimize creativity and leave you open to unforeseen circumstances that get in the way of your quality of life. Practice creates innovation and flushes out the obstacles so you can prepare how to sidestep them if they occur."

If there is one area of life that is definitely like sports, it's PRACTICE AND PREPARATION. People who will scream your name and beg for more like to know that whatever you do in life, you do it with excellence.

Excellence comes from creating good habits in practice and preparation. Just as a football coach or player looks at a playbook and studies film before any game, it is important for you, in your life and business decisions, to study your life playbook that you are forming as you read this book.

I highly recommend that you write your decisions down for each of the areas that I have been talking about in this book. Put them into a "Life Action Plan" journal. I have talked extensively about why you need to have a plan for your life. I want to reinforce the importance of writing your plan down. This will provide a road map for you to stay on course and live your life, while remaining flexible for opportunity and unexpected fun experiences. At the end of the book, there is a list of the key areas that you need to make choices for in your Life Action Plan.

Once you have your Life Action Plan in writing, you then can practice and prepare throughout your life for the path you will take in the pursuit of your ultimate life. Having a Life Action Plan gives you a visual document that you can sit down with on a quarterly to six-month basis, and think about where you are and where you are headed in life. As you look at where you are headed, you can pre-think where you want to be in the future, and look at where you are supposed to be and make changes to your plan if there is a gap. Preparation without practice in life and business limits your creative ideas, and leaves you unprepared for unexpected circumstances that can have a

negative impact on your life. Had you "practiced" what you
"prepared," you would have said, at some point, "What if
we were able to (insert idea)." Or you may say, "You
know, as I think through this, my concern is (insert
concern). If all you do is prepare, you will get caught up in
the details that can deter you from seeing new ideas and
threats to your success.

I recommend this process for any aspect of your life
including, preparing for the college you will attend, the
major you will pick, the interview process when looking for
a job, having kids, choosing a career, opening your own
company, and making all major decisions within that
company. Preparing and practicing will maximize your
success in the most cost-effective and efficient way.

Let me share with you how preparation and practice
have made a huge difference in my life, both personally
and professionally.

In 1996, I directed and planned my first big trade show
and conference for my first association. It went quite well.
We had great attendance compared to their past shows, and
reviews were very positive. I worked from my company's
timeline of "things to do" to plan the event, which was
there before I was hired. I had never planned an event of
this magnitude, so I thought this was the way it was done.
The show went great, but I believed it could have been
much better. I was determined to make 1997 an amazing
expo and conference. Our team went into the planning

process, as we did in 1996, but we bit off more than we could chew. We expanded the expo, increased the amount of educational sessions, and we had a location that put the expo and conference in two different buildings, a few blocks from each other. We had all the pieces to be successful, and we pursued it with the same planning process that we used before. As the show took place, there were a number of hiccups throughout the event that were brought out in our post-show critique. I can remember the post-show critique very vividly with my Board of Directors. There were small details here and there that were missed because we bit off a larger plan than we could pull off with the number of staff that we had. We prepared big, but didn't practice. Had we practiced the event in our minds, over and over in the planning process, we would have seen very clearly we did not have the staff to do what we were planning.

I made a commitment that year that I would never pursue anything that has a large and lasting impact without "practicing" the plan as a part of the process. What I developed as a result, was an event-planning document that became our organization's "playbook." Instead of managing the details by a timeline and checklist, we managed by event. We dedicated a page for every event within the expo and conference, with every minor detail needed for that event to be done with excellence. After putting the playbook together for the meeting, we would meet every month and sometimes twice a month, going through the playbook, event by event. We played out the event in our minds, as if we were actually there. This allowed us to virtually live out and "practice" the event over and over again. Once on site, we would do one last walk through of the playbook to ensure no final questions. Having worked through the playbook twenty plus times before the event ensured that we had thought of every detail related to attendee experience and operational issues. This new process fostered the "What if we could do this?" and "What if this happens?" discussion. I've used this process for every event that I've planned both professionally and personally, and every single one of them has been executed with precision and excellence.

If you are a college student or unemployed looking for a job, how much are you preparing and practicing for the interview process. Your competition is tough in the job market. You have to bring your "A" game to the interview, or you will get looked over. It is imperative that you look at how you dress for the interview, do you know the top fifty interview questions and how you would answer, do you know their company and industry, and do you have a set of five questions for them so they get a true sense that you are very interested in working for them? Employers want to know that you are not just looking for a job, but that you have a desire to make a difference in their company. Interviewing at that level takes preparation and practice.

Consider having a friend sit on the company's website and ask you questions about them, to help you practice answering questions about the company. Have them ask you questions about yourself from the top fifty interview questions. Find someone wanting to scream your name and beg for more to help you in this process.

As I'm writing this book, my wife and I are already practicing retirement. We are a number of years away from retirement, but when we get there, we want to make sure we are prepared and have practiced it so that we have thought through all the things that could have a negative impact on our retirement experience. We have worked through living in a condo, a home, or traveling in an RV. When we travel, do we want to be in an RV, a pop-up camper with an SUV, or stay in hotels? Do we really want a second condo to have a place to stay on vacations and rent out for another retirement revenue stream? Looking at what our monthly expenses will be, how many buckets of retirement income will we need?

As we research and mentally "practice" retirement, it is helping us to "prepare" effectively for retirement. It's those unexpected circumstances that you didn't plan for in life and retirement that cause you to have to work longer or compromise your experience because you deflated your retirement income.

The same holds true for every aspect of your life and business. For any major decisions in your life or business, after you plan and prepare…PRACTICE, PRACTICE, PRACTICE. Through the "mental practice" you will discover new ways to approach your decision, discover what obstacles will get in your way, and become excellent at the execution phase of the decision.

On the following page, I've referred to my "Path to the Ultimate Life" diagram as your center point to prepare, practice, and execute on any life decision, along with the steps to take.

Steps to Effective Preparation and Practice

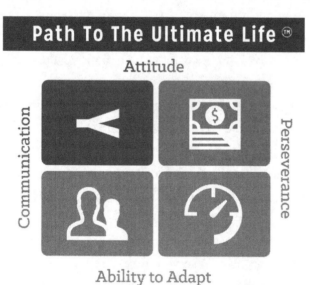

1. What is the objective that you want to accomplish?
2. What are the choices that you need to make to accomplish your objectives?

3. How much money will you need to invest in order to accomplish your objectives?
4. What is your time investment in order to accomplish your objectives?
5. What people do I need to be networked with, or have access to, in order to accomplish my objectives?
6. Do I have the right attitude to be successful pursuing my goals?
7. What changes do I have to adapt to in order to be successful?
8. Am I willing to persevere and commit to whatever it takes?
9. How and what do I have to communicate in order to be successful?
10. Knowing the first nine answers, do I have what it takes?

Use these ten questions for any major decisions. If the answer to number ten is YES, then execute and pursue it with passion. Life demands that you bring your "A" game. If you bring it every day, you will experience a life with more confidence, excitement, energy, and a winning attitude. People can't help but scream your name and beg for more.

Application to the Ultimate Life

Do you feel you adequately prepare and practice for big life decisions?

How often do you actually spend mentally practicing your life choices to ensure excellence in execution?

How can you improve your time spent in practicing life?

Action Steps to the Ultimate Life

Take your next two big life decisions and work through the ten questions on "Steps to Effective Preparation and Practice."

Mentally think through and play out your next big life decision by writing down all of the ideas that you need in order to be successful…as well as obstacles that will prevent your success. Practice until there are no obstacles.

Chapter 16
The Pursuit

"If you don't like your circumstances in life, you are always one decision and three steps from changing your life. The first step you must take is to PURSUE change."

Ahhh...the call to action... the PURSUIT. It is the thing that stops many people from being successful. It's easy to think about your purpose, find your passion and talk it over with people. But once you have done all of the planning, preparing and practicing, you still need to take action...you still need to PURSUE! You need to JUMP!

You need to GO! You need to PUT ACTION TO YOUR WORDS to achieve your ultimate life!

So many things hold people back at this point. Even people who have a solid chance of success sit on their hands because of the fear of failure, their past, and even success. They don't like the thought of the attention that success will bring to them.

If you are in high school and have a college that you want to go to, but think that you can't afford it…try thinking again. Look at the **Path to the Ultimate Life** visual again. If you manage your time, money, people, and choices well, with perseverance, the ability to adapt, good communication, and an awesome attitude, then you can go to any college that you want. That means that YOU make a CHOICE to know what YOU need to do to get in. You hang with PEOPLE who earn the grade point average that you need to earn in order to get into the college that you want to get into. You seek out the scholarships and the funding for the MONEY that you need. You invest the TIME in studying and make the GPA you need to make.

If you are a job seeker and there is a position that you want at a certain level, then you need to make the CHOICE to do what it takes to have the necessary qualifications for that position. Network with PEOPLE in the industry. Have the MONEY to make your bills until an opening becomes available. Invest the TIME in studying that company's business model to wow them in your interview.

If you are a business executive and there is a market or opportunity you want to pursue, the same applies. You must make a smart CHOICE on which market to pursue. You must be willing to invest the MONEY to market your company or yourself. Spend the TIME researching the market and all the angles to maximize your profits. Assemble the PEOPLE that you need in sales, marketing, operations, and production to be successful.

If you are someone who just wants to make a change in your life, then you must be willing to make the CHOICE to do what it takes…invest the TIME necessary, spend or save the MONEY needed, and reach out to the PEOPLE who can help you to make your change.

Change could be moving from renting an apartment to owning a home. Change could be getting out of a toxic relationship. Change could be getting out of debt. Change could be quitting smoking, drugs, or alcohol abuse. Change could be putting your family as your top priority, not working seventy hours a week.

Whatever the change, you need to PURSUE. Take the leap of faith once you have walked through the process that I talked about in the plan, preparation, and practice chapters. Let me forewarn you, once you PURSUE, there WILL be speed bumps. Things that come along that will make you feel discouraged and even want to give up. They may cause you to ask yourself, "Did I make the right choice?"

That is where the four characteristics discussed earlier come into play. No matter whether you are a student wanting to go to a good college, a person seeking a great job, an executive looking to pursue a new market opportunity, or an at-home mom wanting to make a change, you will not succeed if you don't have the perseverance to not give up on your goal. You must have the ability to adapt to the environmental changes that come your way. Surround yourself with the people you need to succeed and communicate your goal well to those in your path.

The ability to pursue with confidence isn't about being 100% sure of success. No one can ever be 100% sure of success. Heck, 50% of businesses started fail within five years. 50% of first marriages end in divorce, and 41% of freshman never graduate college.

In my opinion, the confidence to take the leap of faith and pursue change or a dream in your life is about being 33% planned, prepared, and practiced; 33% sure of your success, 33% sure that you will excel at the four characteristics to do what it takes, and 1% guts to PURSUE. The interesting part is that the 1% is what holds many people back. I say seize the day! The most incredible thing is that you are in absolute control of your choices, time, money, and people, to pursue. The question is, do you have the ability to adapt, the perseverance, a healthy, positive attitude, and the communication skills to do what it takes?

I BELIEVE THAT YOU DO! Everyone is born with the four special characteristics needed to excel in the four areas of choices, money, people, and time. The problem is that life happens, and our bad experiences, the past, and stream of bad choices get in the way of our success. We dig ourselves into a hole and feel helpless, like it's just too deep to dig our way back out.

Listen, the first choice that you need to make is, ENOUGH IS ENOUGH and YOU ARE TIRED OF YOUR CIRCUMSTANCES. Look above your current circumstances and make the choice to make new and better choices for your life. How do you think homeless people become rich, poor people become successful, kids surrounded by horrible circumstances break through and become successful in life? It's because they make a choice to PURSUE a better life. Remember, you don't drown by falling into the water…you drown by staying there.

You've heard some of my stories in each of the previous chapters. I've been through a lot in my life. I've been unemployed, I've wondered if I even had enough money to put food on the table for my family, I've had two friends chip in to pay my mortgage payment, I've experienced the pain of divorce, and I've drowned in a state of bankruptcy. All of these circumstances in my life came about because I did not pursue the right direction with excellence in my choices, people, money, and time. One, or even all of them, were out of alignment.

I remember the day that I decided, NEVER AGAIN. It was the day I chose to pursue bringing all four of the Pillars in my life into alignment, and to pursue the Characteristics with a never quit attitude. It was the summer of 2005. The JaxMetroLive singles ministry was coming to the end of its three-year run of success, and it's time as a full-time venture was ending. It was a moment when I was faced with, "Do I keep running with this opportunity or make another choice?" Taking my family needs in consideration, I had probably stayed in the ministry about a year too long. I had become blinded by the emotions that I had birthed this thing, and it was making such a difference in people's lives. Why shouldn't I continue on? However, the reality of it was, it wasn't financially providing for my family's needs. I came to a fork in the road of a good or bad choice. In the summer of 2005, I made the choice to get back into the corporate world. I sat down and went through the thought process I discussed in the Prepare and Practice chapter. Once I got it all down on paper, I was then disturbed enough about my circumstances to begin PURSUING my future.

I jumped, with a huge leap of faith, into pursuing a corporate position. There were only two companies in my city that even did what I was great at and had plenty of experience for. Neither of them had any openings, so I made another good choice, to make another leap of faith and pursue a financial planning career. I had experience with financial planning from early in my work life. I landed a job with a major financial planning company, and within sixty days of working in this new position, I received the call I spoke of earlier in the book, from the one company in the huge city of Jacksonville, who could offer me a position in the field that I wanted to enter... and I was very good at. I made the leap to pursue that opportunity, and have helped my current company experience amazing growth since 2006.

What I learned was that once you start pursuing opportunities and pursuing them with excellence, people want to scream your name and beg for more, because they see you as a doer...someone who makes things happen. By pursuing with a passion to help people, not to sell them something, people are drawn to help you because you have no agenda to gain something in return.

The moral of this chapter is, don't be afraid to pursue. Seize the moment and go! The ultimate life awaits your arrival. Remember the **Path to the Ultimate Life** visual in everything that you do.

Application to the Ultimate Life

What do you fear most about pursuing your dreams?
If everything were in alignment, describe what your ultimate life would look like?
What lessons have you learned about making the leap to

pursue big decisions in your past?

What do you think you should NOT do when pursuing big decisions?

Action Steps to the Ultimate Life

Write down the life-changing thing that you want to pursue in the next 6 months?

What two steps are you going to take in the next 30 days to pursue the big decision above?

Chapter 17
It's Time to Party

"It's your life "party" that refreshes, reenergizes, and refuels your soul and passion for life. "Party" your way, and do it often."

WOW! So you have made it to chapter 17, my favorite chapter...It's Time to Party! You have accomplished so much at this stage of the game. Let's look at what you have learned so far:

- The four main things that will impact every decision you make to live the ultimate life

- The four characteristics you need to have to excel in the four areas of decision-making
- You are your own Chief Energy Officer
- You own your decisions and your future
- You have defined your purpose
- You have discovered your passions
- You have defined your principles to live by
- You have set your priorities in order
- You have surrounded yourself with the right people
- You've discovered how to become FREE of your past
- You have planned the path that you want to take
- You have prepared and practiced for your success
- You have paused and meditated on your plan
- You have made the leap to pursue and succeed

That is such an amazing accomplishment to have worked through all of that for your life! NOW IT'S TIME TO PARTY AND CELEBRATE the victories, freedom, and ultimate life you will be experiencing along the way! Now, before you run off and say, "Now Tom, I'm not the partying type" or "Tom I'm over forty years old. I gave up partying years ago." Let me define partying for you. My definition of partying is, "doing that which gives you the most fulfillment to refuel, reenergize, and refresh your life to keep up the pursuit of your purpose and passions for the ultimate life."

For some, that may be reading a novel on a beach

somewhere. For someone else, it may be taking a cruise. For others, it may be hiking through the Grand Canyon. For my wife and I, we love a good cruise with a great nightclub. We love great music and dancing. Dancing allows us to let loose, while also feeding our souls with a good time, doing what we love. We also love the opportunities that a cruise provides to see many unique places in one travel experience. You can experience and see so many amazing things and meet new people. That is what feeds us as a couple and refreshes us to meet the demands that we have chosen with our life goals.

If you want people to scream your name and beg for more, then you need to find what your party is. People from all types of life and personalities are drawn to people who know how to enjoy life at any level. If you are not a people person, I would encourage you to get out of your comfort zone, find your "party," and experience it with others who enjoy the same "party" as you. You can leverage your party activity to expand your network of people who could expand your life opportunities, or your talents can help to expand theirs. Remember, the ultimate life is as much about giving as it is receiving.

So what is your "party?" Have you discovered it? If you haven't, you need to find out what your "party" is and seek to do it now, and do it as often as time and money allows. Doing your "party" will refresh your soul. It will provide enjoyment, happiness, and a level of positive energy so that nothing negative can penetrate your life. Will negative things come into your life? Absolutely. Misery loves company, but it will not dictate your life. When your glass of life is so full of positive things and emotions, there is no room for negative things.

I have sat and talked with so many people in my life, and I hear this common theme…"I can't wait to retire to start pursuing my passion in life." I see so many people who are living to work, when they should be working to LIVE! Remember, work is simply the financing mechanism that brings the funding for you to pursue the things that you enjoy the most. If you are not able to pursue them right now and you would like to, then you need to go back to the **Path to the Ultimate Life** visual and study it. Work through your choices, money, people, and time decisions, to put you on a path to being able to do "your party" on a regular basis, so you can experience life today.

If you need a motivator to start now, go back to the life exercise and look at how many white blocks you have left. If you are younger, don't wait until there aren't many left to decide to live your life. If you are older, get moving now. Every day you wait is another set of blocks being colored in, without you experiencing the life you desire to have.

Another step that I want you to take as you pursue your "party" is to take pictures…and take a lot of them as you visit amazing places and enjoy incredible experiences. Each year, look back at your year of pictures and rejoice in those experiences, the people you have met, and the fun you have had. Technology has played a huge role in our life, in being able to see the incredible moments that we regularly enjoy, every day. There are online programs called Printagram and PosterMyWall, which in a few short steps, allow you to select a 20" x 30" poster, upload 50+ pictures from your Instagram or Facebook account, and have a glossy, high quality poster mailed right to your house.

This past year, my wife and I created two posters- one with the pictures of us over the past two years, and another poster of our favorite pictures of our kids. We hung those on our wall going up our stairs to our bedroom, so that every time we go up or down the stairs, we are looking at the most incredible experiences that we have had over the last two years. We have committed to changing one out each year to update the wall and keep it fresh. Staying consistently happy throughout your life is about being able to remember the good times you have had, and smile at them on a bad day to remind you that your life really is fun. One bad day or experience doesn't define your life...don't let it.

You see, we get burned out in life because we can come to a place where we forget that our life is really pretty good. Having the visual documentation on the walls that you pass by every day helps you to remember how awesome your life really is, and the people in your like will keep you on fire, wanting to experience more of life. That is why programs like Facebook and Instagram are so amazing…they document and touch on the positive emotions that you have experienced, so that you can go back and see that life is really pretty good.

Since PosterMyWall allows you to upload pictures from any of your friends' Facebook photo galleries, you can document a friend's amazing life events as well, and have it mailed directly to them as a gift. We had a poster designed in a matter of minutes, documenting a friend's previous two years with her best Facebook pictures, and we had it delivered to her new place as a house warming gift. You would have thought we had given her a million dollars. She loved it because it brought back so many great emotions and memories with her boyfriend. They loved it so much that they put it on the wall right by their front door, so they could see it every day…coming in and out of their house.

A big key to having an awesome life is remembering consistently how awesome your life has been up to that moment. Without the cool experiences being shown to us on a constant basis, we can easily lose sight of how exciting our life actually is.

Make a commitment to find your "party." Document it with pictures or videos, and use them in a way that helps you to remember how great your life is. Don't leave them on your camera or in a computer folder, or put them in some album that will never be opened. Share those photos in such a way that you stay tuned into how good the "party" of your life really is.

If your pictures and memories are ones that you would prefer to leave behind, then go back to my **Path to the Ultimate Life** visual and rethink how you need to change your decisions, money, time, and people. Start making a poster of pictures today that you would love to have hanging on your wall, making you smile every time you pass it.

Refresh, refuel, and reenergize your life today. Don't let a spot on your chest, a bad mammogram, a sudden heart attack, or a life altering accident be the reason that you decide to find your "party." Find it starting tomorrow, and do it often. Find others who enjoy the same "party" and experience it with them. Your health and your soul will thank you for it years later.

Application to the Ultimate Life

What is your "party" that refreshes, refuels, and reenergizes your life?

What keeps you from experiencing your "party" as much as you would like?

How often do you feel you need to experience your "party" to keep your life refreshed, refueled, and reenergized?

What changes do you need to make to start experiencing your "party" this week?

Action Steps to the Ultimate Life

Write down the changes you will make this week toward pursuing your "party."

Write down how many times you are going to commit to experiencing your "party" over the next year.

Chapter 18
The Power of Networking

"Every hand you shake has the power
to change your life."

The power of networking can transform your personal life, career, and business, if you take the time to master what it's all about. In my opinion, networking is one of the greatest life skills never taught to us as children or business professionals, yet we are called upon to do it all the time. Every day, both personally and professionally, we have opportunities and challenges that are presented to us. Each day, people who could enhance those opportunities or bring a solution to our challenges walk into our life. Most people never even know how others can help them because they never bother to engage them in a conversation that would lead them to know how they can help. With networking, most conversations are never about if someone can help you right now. Most conversations are about getting to know someone and then remembering what you have learned about them in your mental database for that moment of time in the future when they can help you or someone you know.

Networking, as defined by Webster's Dictionary, is "a supportive system of sharing information and services among individuals or groups having a common interest." Today, we live in a personal and business climate, in which the demands on us as individuals can be almost overwhelming. It moves at light speed where change is constant, and the ability to keep up with it all seems impossible. With this fast-paced and changing environment in a world where we can never really "know it all," why would you try and go it alone?

The first key to any advancement or growth in personal life, professional development, or business is surrounding yourself with a constantly growing network of people who can provide you or your organization with help, at any given time. It's what this entire book is about. To build a network of people effectively, you have to understand the art of networking.

The way to build a network is not about entering into a conversation to see what someone can do for you. The first step in networking is to get to know people, and then see how you can help them. Through that conversation, they will ultimately share how they may be able to help you, in some way.

I had the fortunate pleasure of attending a conference a few years ago where I heard an amazing speaker. She has an incredible story about how learning and using the art of networking helped her to rise through the ranks, from a 19-year old intern at the White House to the White House Director of Events and Meetings at age 25. Ultimately, she was producing every event that President Clinton was involved with. She stated over and over that, while she was working her way up through the ranks, whenever she would enter any social event and meet people, her number one question was, "How can I help you?" I've learned quickly that when people get to know you over time, they size you up, trying to gauge whether or not you are a taker or a giver. If people brand you as a "giver," then they want to be around you more because you aren't seen as someone always wanting something from them. If you are deemed a "taker," people don't necessarily make an effort to hang with you or want to help you because they feel like you will ask them for something else. If you want people to scream your name and beg for more, make sure you are a "giver of life," not a "taker of life," in the world of networking.

People WANT to help givers.

In the world of networking, people will always remember those who have helped them to be successful, and typically they are more than willing to return the favor. The key to this element is that you help them to achieve their goal without any expectation of a return favor…that makes it genuine.

As I stated earlier, networking is about a connection to an individual or group of people who, through your positive relationship, can help you at any given moment in time. The first key to focus on is the "positive" relationship. Most people don't like to be around people who bring a negative emotion to the relationship. People like to help people who are bringing a positive vibe- those who make progress going forward in life or business. No one enjoys listening, in any kind of meeting, to the person who always says… "Well, that's not going to work, and let me tell you why." I'm not saying that no one should ever question something, but there are people who question everything for the purpose of keeping things the way they are or out of fear of change. These are people that you want to steer clear of. They are disruptive to your life and progress in achieving your goals. That's not to say that you never hang out with them…you just don't bring them into your inner circle that is helping you to meet your life or business goals.

The second key is "the connection" to an individual or

group of common interest. Networking is all about the connection. There are two types of connections: a connection to you, and a connection between that person and someone you know who could use their expertise. I have gained more favor in life within my network by being a master connector. When I'm talking to people, I always get their business card. As I talk to them, I write down on their card how they may help someone I know someday. I make sure that I put them in my personal database, so they are always in my phone. As life happens and people around me talk about opportunities or challenges happening, people love it when you are able to say, "Hey, I know this person who can help you. Let me connect you two tomorrow and see how they can help." Their eyes light up and they get a big smile. This is especially true if it's a business referral. Leverage the fundamentals of networking from this chapter to help yourself, but more importantly, how to connect people who need each other.

The key to building your network is in your common interests or needs. The common areas of interest or needs are important because they give you the basis for getting to know one another. If you have nothing in common, the conversation will be short. In networking, you want to focus on areas that allow for depth of conversation so you can get to know someone well.

I heard a phrase once that changed my life with regards to relying on people and building trust. It goes like this:

- You should never trust someone more than you know them.
- You should never rely on someone more than you can trust them.
- You should never commit to someone more than you can rely on them.

I see people every day who trust someone with something important when they barely know them. I see people who rely on others way more than they can trust them, and they commit to people who they can't rely on very much. It is important for the success of your life that you pay close attention to the three statements above. Make sure you really know someone as much as you trust them; rely on someone only as much as you trust them; and, never commit to someone that you can't rely on.

When it comes to looking at the common areas to build your network, some groups to think about are:

- Those with similar interests
- Individuals with similar needs
- Same age range
- Mentors
- Same stages of life (married, single, parents, business owner, etc.)
- Career type
- Spheres of Influence

Spheres of influence are a really big one because these are people who know many people and are influential within their network. A key strategy within online networking through Twitter is to not necessarily have 10,000 average followers, but to have 100 highly influential followers who have 10,000 followers of their own…that taps you into 100,000 people! The same holds true in your face-to-face network. Focus on building a network of people, who will open up other networks for you.

Another major key to networking is to know your personality and the personalities of others. To maximize your success at networking, you need to take the time to understand the strengths and weaknesses of the four different personality types. The most successful networkers that I've ever experienced have always been able to identify what makes people tick within minutes of talking to them. Knowing this allows them to know "how" to talk to people. Some people want to hear vision…some want to hear about your family…some want to hear the bottom line. Everyone has a way of talking that causes them to engage in your presence the most. Think about it. It's like walking into a room full of people who speak different languages. If you walk over to a group of four people who speak Chinese and you are trying to speak English, you aren't going to get very far. However, if you begin to speak Chinese to them, you draw an instant connection that brings them closer to you. The same holds true with personality types. If you have someone who puts a lot of focus on the details of a situation and you start talking about a big vision, then you've lost them. If you have someone who is a quiet type and very personal and you start prying into them with overly personal questions, then you've lost them.

The more you can understand who people are, the better you will know "how" to talk to them to get them to open up, and to draw them closer to you. There are many resources and books that you can access to study the four personality types. I would recommend tapping into them soon. With that said, let's take a brief look at the four personality types.

The four personality types have all been characterized in many ways, including Greek words, shapes, animals, and colors. They all break down to four:

- Life of the Party
- Decision Maker
- Perfectionist
- Can't We All Just Get Along

Here is a short list of strengths and weaknesses of each personality type:

Life of the Party
- **Strengths:** Talkative, Energetic, Creative, Starts Everything, Lives in the Present

- **Weaknesses:** Exaggerates, Undisciplined, Doesn't Listen Well, Doesn't Follow Through

Decision Maker
- **Strengths:** Born Leader, Goal-Oriented, Delegates Well, Can Run Anything
- **Weaknesses:** Bossy, Impatient, Manipulative, Knows Everything

Perfectionist
- **Strengths:** Deep Thoughts, Persistent, Sacrifices for Everyone, Loves Analysis Work
- **Weaknesses:** Not People-Oriented, Critical of Others, Sees the Negative, Not a Very Tactful Communicator

Why Can't We All Just Get Along
- **Strengths:** Easy- Going, Consistent, Avoids Conflict, Good Listener
- **Weaknesses:** Not Self-Motivated, Avoids Responsibility, Resists Change, Would Rather Watch

Everyone typically has one personality type that is their dominating style, with a secondary style that complements it. I found this out in my early thirties, when I had just moved in with a new roommate. One day he came home and told me that he had just taken this personality test and he shared it with me. He said it would be interesting for me to take one to see how our lifestyles might clash. At first I was hesitant, but a few days later I clicked the link and took the test. When I got the instant result I was astonished and shocked. It stated that I was the "Life of the Party" type with "Decision Maker" tendencies. When I read through the one page summary description of my personality traits it freaked me out. It said I was "Captain Wild Child:" starts everything, but finishes nothing; disorganized and talks a lot. These were just a few of the many descriptions. I was like…"THIS IS ME AND I'M IN TROUBLE!"

It was very important for me at this very moment in my life to learn this because I had just landed my first CEO position with a non-profit trade association in charge of three companies with over $3,000,000 in annual revenue and $4,000,000 in the bank. I basically said to myself, "If I don't make some changes in myself, I'll be fired in the first year."

You see, it is important to look in the mirror to see yourself and your personality so you can learn who you are at the core of your being. The biggest mistake anyone makes is saying, "That personality test is a lie. That's not me." What you are saying is, "I don't like who I am." If you want to be all that you can be in life, then you need to be real with who you are. This will help you to make the changes in your life needed to strengthen the areas that will hold you back, or it will make you into someone that people don't want to listen to or be around.

After reading the report, I immediately analyzed myself and implemented changes to help me be more effective in life: I started using a day timer and checklists to ensure that I don't forget details; I made sure to not say a word until someone finished their story; and, I try not to start any projects unless there are resources and time available to do them effectively. I looked in the mirror, took ownership of who I was, and made changes to help me be more effective and successful in life. I will admit, even today, I'm not perfect in these areas, but I'm a work in progress. If you are not careful, your natural weak tendencies will come out of nowhere. It's why I have always surrounded myself with people who have strengths in my areas of weakness.

When looking at personalities, you need to discern whether the traits that you, or anyone else has, are a natural trait or a learned trait. Natural traits are typically your strengths that you do with no problem. Learned traits are things that you have done to strengthen your weaknesses as I stated above. I am naturally a disorganized person. If you looked at how I manage my life, you would think I'm a very organized person. Organization is a learned trait for me. The goal is to leverage the strengths that you have naturally, and learn how to strengthen your areas of weakness. If you do play to your strengths and improve on them, or hire people for your weaknesses, you will be a person who will be successful in many areas of your life.

When I talk about these various personality traits with others, the first thing they say to me is, "Wow. Now I know why he or she reacts this way when I do this." When you know someone's personality traits, it will help you to understand why they respond or react in a certain way, given your interaction with them. This helps you to act or communicate in such a way so people will hear what you need them to hear.

Let me give you an example that I've personally witnessed. Let's say you are a "life of the party" type like me, who can more or less "wing it" during the work day. You can run with little organization, but not too much. You are always flexible and can react instantly when people put things on your desk to do. Let's say you work with a "perfectionist," who is highly organized with their day…everything has its place and will get done as it comes up on their written schedule. If you walk into the "perfectionist's" office and drop a project of any type on their desk that has to be done sooner rather than later, that situation is not going to go down well- not because they don't want to or can't get it done, but because you gave it to them in a way that totally conflicts with their personality. To effectively fit into their mind-set, you should have walked in and asked them if they had some time to help you on a project, talk to them about when they might be able to discuss it, and then get the project on their calendar to go over it and plan it out. In doing that, you just spoke their "language" and they respected you for it, as well as responded very favorably.

You see, the reason many people don't want to scream someone's name and beg for more isn't because they dislike them. They just don't like the way that they treat them, because they don't respect their time and space by speaking their "language." We tend to speak and treat people like we are talking to someone who thinks and acts just like us...big mistake. You have to talk to people in such a way that they understand what you want to communicate and are asking them to do.

The last key is to understand that networking is continuous and perpetual...it never stops. Every time you enter a room or shake a hand, it's an opportunity to meet someone who may be the connection that you need for a job, a referral, or help getting into the next door. In every social situation, there is someone in the room that you need to meet that you did not know.

I know what many of you are saying at this point, "But Tom, I'm not a people person. I'm uncomfortable in a room full of people, especially people I don't know." Let me assure you that many people you may meet in that room also feel the same way. So my encouragement to you is to step out of your comfort zone and introduce yourself. At the end of this chapter, I will share a simple system for you to use, on how to start up and move a conversation forward with anyone.

A few other keys that you need to know about being a power networker are:

Be Viral

A ton of networking and connection takes place online with LinkedIn, Facebook, Instagram, and Twitter. I've heard stories of someone seeing six-figures of business come their way, simply because they sent a positive tweet to the CEO of a company whose produce they used. The CEO responded back, and the next thing you know, they connected and they are now seeing business from that company. Had they called the CEO, they would never have gotten past the receptionist, but Twitter and other social media tools allow you to bypass the gatekeeper and be heard by everyone.

Minimize and Eliminate Time Wasters

Your time is valuable, and while you are talking to someone who has no interest in who you are, you are missing out on connecting with someone who may be a vital connection to your life. Remember, there are people who network simply to empty their bucket of drama on others and talk about other people. Minimize your quality time with these people.

Listen With Your Heart and Often

Simply put, be genuine and hear people's

stories. Don't fake who you are. Be real and transparent. When you open up your heart to people and listen to theirs, then the ultimate connections are made.

Always be Aware of Where You Are, Who You Are With, and Who Could Be Watching

There's a time and place for everything. In the world of networking, you want to make sure that you aren't letting your hair down in an environment that could have negative consequences for some future opportunities that you may have. Almost anything you do out in the open, and sometimes behind closed doors, will be documented by someone standing from afar with their phone...next thing you know, you are a feature on the internet. Be wise to not do something that, if seen by many in the open space, would have a big negative impact on your personal life or career.

Be Curious

Ask lots of questions and get to know others. People LOVE to talk about themselves and what they do for a living, their family, and hobbies. They love to brag about themselves. Leverage that to your advantage. Share your wisdom when asked, but only when asked. Always ask people for permission to give them feedback. Don't force your opinions and help people to create ideas and solutions. Don't be afraid to challenge ideas.

Remember and Use Names

People love to hear other people call them by name. If you don't think so, try saying, "Thank you INSERT NAME," the next time you purchase something. You will see the person smile. Calling someone by name says, "You were important enough for me to remember your name." This is especially true when you meet someone for the first time and don't see them again for a while. If, at the next interaction, you immediately call them by name, that's very impressive to them. A good idea is to get a picture with them and their business card, and upload their information into your phone with a picture of their face for future reference. Use technology in networking to help you be impressive.

Not Everyone Will Like You

Remember that we are all different. Not everyone likes or gets along with certain personalities. There are differing opinions. Many people have a past history that just won't allow them to like who you are, and some are going to be jealous or envious of you for whatever reason. Getting along with others takes grace, patience, and forgiveness. I will say this, though, if numerous people consistently don't like you, have negative things to say about you, and you are always on the outside looking in, then you need to take a look in the mirror. You may need to make some personal adjustments as we spoke about before. However, if a small percentage of people in your life don't like you, don't let it deter you...move on, they are most likely time wasters. My motto is, if 10% of the people in your life are not indifferent to who you are and what you stand for, then you probably aren't growing, innovating, and pushing the envelope enough...you are just trying to make everyone happy and go along with the crowd. You are not called to make everyone happy...you are called to make a difference.

Everybody is Somebody

Always assume that you need to meet a person and never underestimate who you are shaking hands with. That person could know the person who is your next boss or next big client. Always treat everyone you meet with respect and honesty, as if they are the person who knows someone else you need to meet.

Business Cards

Like the American Express commercial says, "Never leave home without it." Business cards are how people remember you once you leave their presence. As you develop your business cards, think about having a QR code so people can scan it with their phone...this way you are in their phone immediately. If you are unemployed, a college student, or working for a company who doesn't provide you with business cards, then have some made up for yourself with your contact information on them and your own "self title". The best one that I ever saw was a friend of mine who gave herself the title, "Your Go-To Girl." She was saying to anyone that she gave her card to, "If you need something, I can help." That's creative and memorable to anyone that she gives that card to.

Now that you know the keys to networking, I want to share with you a simple system for connecting with people once you have entered the room. It's a nice mental system of networking communication that I learned from a colleague who has since passed on. As you approach someone at the bar, networking event, church event, or small group, you have just reached out your hand and said typically, "Hi, my name is….." Most people don't know what comes next. Here is what comes next…it's called F.O.R.M.:

Family

Everyone likes to talk about their family, so you start with simple questions like:

- Where are you originally from?
- Does your family live here?
- How long have you and your Spouse/Partner lived here?
- What are your kids into at their ages?

At some point, you then will transition into:

Occupation

Most people like to talk about what they do, whether it's good or bad, so you move into questions related to their work:

- So what do you do for a living?
- How is the economy in that industry?
- What are the major challenges a company like yours is seeing right now?
- What do you like the most about your job?

Recreation

People have passions or outside activities that they love:

- When you aren't at work, what do you like to do?
- What do you like best about that activity?
- Are you a sports fan?
- Who is your favorite team?

My Time

After talking with someone about their Family, Occupation, and Recreation, now it's **"My Time."** The problem is that you never get to "MY TIME" because you spent so much time letting the other person do what they like to do most...talk about themselves.

Your letting them talk so much about themselves leaves them thinking that you are this incredible listener,

and an awesome person that they just
met. BOOM! Connection and lasting impression made.

Again, networking is a life skill everyone should
master. Start working on your ability to connect. You never
know which hand you shake that will change your life
forever in the future. I have a book full of stories about how
people I met through networking have helped my life, or
people who I have connected and who have helped each
other. A hand I shook in 1995, belonged to a man who
called me in 2005 to ask me if I would come be his #2
person in his company to eventually take over as CEO
when he retired in two years. While interviewing me, he
said he always remembered how passionate my ideas were
when he met me 10 years earlier…I was his only call to be
his #2 person. That is the power of networking. Learn to be
a power networker and connector of people, and those
around you will scream your name louder than you could
ever imagine and beg for more.

Application to the Ultimate Life

What do you fear most about networking with people you
don't know?
What personality type are you?
What do you feel are your strengths and weaknesses as a
person, professional, and a friend?
What personality type rubs you the wrong way?

What are the areas that you need to improve on to help you be a more effective networker and connector of people?

Action Steps to the Ultimate Life

Make a list of people you need to network with and groups you need to join.

Take a personality test to find out who you are.

Look at your list of strengths and weaknesses and make a list of action steps to help you strengthen your areas of weakness.

Order your business cards if you don't have any.

Commit to networking at least once a month with some group in your local area.

Chapter 19
Your People Must be Diverse

"To maximize your opportunities and quality of life, it's important that you open up to diverse groups of people at all levels. Everyone has something good to offer in your life."

We all know that the topic of diversity brings with it a ton of emotion, politics, and differences in opinion. This chapter is not going to seek to solve all of the socio-economic issues that exist and which drive most discussions on diversity. What it is going to focus on is the human element of diversity.

As we come upon people who are different from ourselves, we all have a choice to either be respectful of and treat others with human decency, no matter who they may be, or, to treat others as if they are different. That is where hate and negative things CAN come into play. I'm going to encourage you to see everyone that you meet in life just like yourself. Treat them like another human being and respect their differences. Treat them as you would want them to treat you. Understand that they are someone's son, daughter, father or mother. They are a human being, first and foremost...different, second.

All you have to do to see diversity is watch television, walk outside, or read any number of magazines. Our society today is a melting pot of people. People who think, act, and speak differently. Diversity comes in many shapes, sizes, and colors. If you live the average life span of 79 years, you are going to experience people of many religions, skin colors, genders, ages, nationalities, and thought processes.

They all bring a different skill set, skill levels, opinions, and opportunities to your life. It is very important for you to know that you need to build a life of diversity if you are to achieve a great quality of life. To see the diversity, take a look at the latest 2010 census data of the population of the United States:

Gender (U.S.):
51% Male
49% Female

Age (U.S.):
34%   Under 18
30%   25 - 44
23%   45 - 65
13%   65 +

Ethnic Groups (U.S.):
72%   White American
13%   African Americans
4.8%   Asian Americans
1.0%   Native Americans
0.2%   Native Hawaiian
6.2%   Some other ethnic group

Religion (World):
32%   Christian
23%   Islam
16%   Unaffiliated
15%   Hinduism
7%   Buddhism
6%   Fold Religions
1%   Other

My point of sharing this data is to show you that we no longer live in a world where there is one kind of people who think, live, or act the same way. You live in a country as well as a world that is very diverse. You need to learn to be open to other people's thinking and ideas. That doesn't mean that you accept their thinking, it simply means that you understand that not everyone thinks like you, and that you respect others rights to think differently. Remember, there are a lot of people all around you who look at you thinking the same thing you think about them..."I can't believe he/she thinks like that!"

By becoming more accepting of a diverse set of people in your life, if frees you to explore other cultures, other ways of thinking, and a more stress-free life.

Instead of looking at someone as being different, because of their religion, gender, or skin color, remember that they have a family just like you. They have a mother. They have a father. They may have kids. They have friends. They work for a living. Most importantly, they are a human being, who is just trying to make it in this world…just like you. Just because they don't look, act, or think like you, doesn't make them worse than you, it just makes them different.

Being a different skin color, religion, or nationality shouldn't be a reason for you to disengage someone from your life. You need to be welcoming and engaging to everyone around you. Those you should think about disengaging in your life should be those who don't stand for the same positive principles that you have in your life, and those who bring a negative impact on your life in one of the four keys areas of choices, money, time, and people you hang with.

I encourage you not to judge people on first sight, but to get to know their story. Everyone has a story and a path of decisions that has brought them to any given moment in life. Everyone has a past filled with good and ugly experiences that have shaped their life up to this point. If a particular person is down on their luck or is close to giving up hope, they may need someone just like you to enter their life, to empower them, and speak truth and hope into their life.

I've witnessed many people in my own life that made prejudgments about people before they were able to actually meet them. Once they got to know who they were and what their life story was, they had a totally different opinion of them.

Don't let diversity cause you to be a divider of people. Let it cause you to be a lover of people of all types and one who brings them together for good. Remember my chapter on networking? Take that chapter and use it as a guide to reach out and get to know others in your local community or industry who aren't like you. As your network of diverse people grows, you will see your life begin to grow.

Application to the Ultimate Life

What do you fear about being around people who aren't like you?

What were you told by your parents about people who aren't like you? Do you still believe them?

If you were to look at 100 people you see over the course of a year, are they a diverse group in age, color, religion, nationality, or thinking?

Why do you feel people are so divided over the differences in others?

Action Steps to the Ultimate Life

Take the time to expand your network into a new diverse group of people within the next 30 days.

Write down three things that you need to change about your thinking to help you create more diversity in your life.

Chapter 20
Identify Your Threats

"No matter what goals you are pursuing in life, there will always be threats to your success. Almost every threat can be prepared to minimize its impact on your success."

Most people wouldn't think about spending the time to think about the threats to the quality of life that you are striving for. Threats are typically things that you do not see coming because you aren't looking for them. Yet almost every threat to your quality of life can typically be seen, and in a lot of cases, prevented, or at least minimized. That doesn't mean that they can always be prevented, but if you can identify a threat before it has the opportunity to manifest itself, you can have a plan in place to minimize its impact on your life.

When most people decide on a goal or purpose they want to obtain, they just decide and go without doing much thinking on what could prevent their goal from happening. Along the way, they encounter numerous frustrating obstacles that are speed bumps in their plan. Frustration occurs from not having thought through the path that you are taking to reach your goal and asking, "Along my journey, what will be all the obstacles from people or unforeseen events that will get in my way?" Asking this question is important because if you know the obstacles that will get in your way, then you don't see the world as working against you because you know these things are most likely going to occur.

So as you look at your situation, where you are in life, and where you are headed, what are all of the threats that can keep you from meeting your goals on time? You need to think for a few moments about threats to any major decisions in your life, including:

- Job changes
- Interviewing for a job
- Getting married
- Having a child

- Having another child
- Dating someone
- I'm divorced…when do I start dating again?
- Going on a big family vacation

These, and many other goals in your life, have the opportunity to derail, or not occur at all because of unforeseen events that take place in the process. The reason they are not seen coming is because you didn't take the time to think about what could happen along the way to your goal. What could prevent your goals from happening like you want? You need to think about that. Think about it with people close to you, who know where you want to go and have some life experience in that area. Write down any event, good or bad, that could prevent or derail your goal. Then start thinking through solutions to ensure that you minimize or eliminate their impact.

My wife and I sit down at least every couple of months over dinner and walk through the conversation of threats on any number of goals in our life. Whether it's a vacation, investing money, or plans in our businesses, we chat consistently about "What are we not thinking of that can get in the way of our plans?"

I will use the element of retirement as an example because it is probably one of the most important goals in life that anyone should have at any age. That's right…any age. Why? Because as I said in my planning chapter, if you take 100 people at age 25, and look at them when they are 65, 66% of them will have become reliant on other people for housing, transportation, food, and health care. They have lost their independence. Think about it…you graduated college at some point, or began working in your career, and you work all your life to get to 65, just to end up having little to live on. Most people end up this way because no one ever had the serious conversation with them about the "threats" to their plan for retirement. There are life events and people that will happen in your life which will keep you from saving enough money to one day have the choice to just sit back and enjoy the fruits of your life-long labor.

When you finish reading this book, I never want you to say later on in life at retirement, "How did I get to this point?" Retirement is a decision that is fully impacted by the items in four Paths to the Ultimate Life, as I discussed in chapter 2, and seen below:

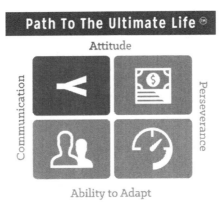

In your life, the four things that will keep you from retiring will be your decisions, how you spend and invest your money, the people you surround yourself with, and how you spend your time. I didn't figure this all out until I was in my late 40's. I can remember sitting down one day, looking out to age 65, and asking myself, "What will my life be like when I'm within reach of 65?" I see so many people who are in their late 50's who will not retire with a good standard of living because they didn't think through the threats to their retirement and plan for them. Other thoughts that go through my head are:

- What will my expenses be at retirement?
- How much money will I need on an annual basis?
- How do I plan so I have enough money, so as to not let my fixed income at retirement prevent me from doing cool stuff?
- What types of unexpected financial expenses will happen after retirement that we need to plan for?

All of these questions were rolling through my mind as I started looking into how to fully fund our retirement. Oh, did you hear me right? I said FULLY fund. That means that you are investing money each month in a variety of different ways to create "buckets of money," so that not one bucket of money, if you were to lose it, can have a negative impact on your standard of living at retirement.

When you reach retirement, you need to either be working, or have money "working for you."

As soon as I started going through this process, I thought to myself, "I wish someone had told me this when I was in my early 20's!" You know why? Because I just recently looked at my earnings record since I was 18 from my online social security account. Had I started putting just five percent of my gross pay away each year from age 25 to age 65, at a reasonable mutual fund interest rate, I would have $1,200,000 at age 65 to retire on. That was from only putting away 5%. If you plan and prepare, almost everyone can learn to live without 5% of your income to prepare for the future. This doesn't even count any money that your company may invest in retirement for you. For this reason, I encourage anyone who works for a company that has a matching fund retirement program, to maximize the amount they will match. Years later, you will be loving life, while watching your pot of money grow.

The moral of this story is, no matter how old you are, start thinking about how much you need at retirement to live the quality of life that you want to live, and start saving AS SOON AS POSSIBLE. The second moral is to think in terms of "buckets of money." When we walked through our plan, we decided we would have a small bucket coming from social security, and larger buckets coming from permanent life insurance, equity investments in mutual funds, and rental income from a vacation property.

Between those four buckets, we could fund our lifestyle at retirement. You need to look at your options with a planner, and decide what your buckets of money will be, and start funding them soon. The amount of money it takes to retire goes up dramatically as you get older.

Now that I've shared our thought process about retirement, let's get back to the discussion of threats to our retiring on time, and having enough money to retire in the fashion that we desire. As my wife and I sat down one night, we started making a list of all the things that could threaten our retirement. They included the following:

- Sudden disability
- Daughters' weddings
- Downturn in the economy
- Unexpected death of one of us
- Unforeseen expenses
- Health care expenses
- Automobiles breaking and/or needing a new one
- Getting fired or down-sized from a job
- Inability to make monthly investment payments
- Needing to pay for, or care for, a parent when they are older

These are just a few of the many that came up. I bet you saw daughters' weddings and thought, "How is that a threat?" Anything that can deter you from achieving a purpose or goal is a threat…even if it's an awesome event. The reality of it is, weddings are expensive, and if you haven't planned on $20,000 to come out of your savings, or you don't have it, then you may be tempted to tap into your retirement fund to make sure your child has their big wedding day. That can delay retirement, so it is a threat that you need to plan for. Threats are not just negative or bad events. Threats are both good and bad events in your life that can keep you from reaching your goal on time.

As I stated in my planning, preparation, and practice chapters, the great thing about pre-thinking your threats with any decision, is that you have the time to make a plan to eliminate or minimize their impact. Through my wife and I looking at our threats, we were able to put into place the following solutions:

- Begin to market for speaking engagements to earn the extra money that we would need to fund retirement and savings.
- Invest in life insurance in case of dying too soon or living too long.
- Start funding an IRA for both of us.
- Purchase disability insurance, in case one of us becomes disabled.
- Get annual physicals to find out any health issues, before they become serious and expensive.
- Ensure that our car's oil and other items are

changed and checked regularly, so no automobile problems come out of nowhere (Auto repairs are way more expensive than oil changes every three months.)

- Put a savings account in place for weddings and unforeseen expenses.
- Invest most of our money in investments that aren't driven by the volatility of the stock market.

You see, once you have your threats on paper, you can put solutions in place to help minimize the negative impact that events or people can have on your goals. Having the solutions in your back pocket will make people want to scream your name and beg for more because when you have solutions already figured out for threats, you are more confident and your goals are securely met. People have confidence in people who they see consistently meeting their goals through well-thought-out plans.

Take threats to your goals in life seriously. Don't wing it. You will save time and money because you have taken the time to think about the solutions to unforeseen threats to your destination.

Application to the Ultimate Life

What threats do you see getting in the way of your personal goals?

What threats do you see getting in the way of your professional goals?
What outside forces are in your life right now and are making it hard for you to achieve your goals?

Action Steps to the Ultimate Life

Write down each threat that you feel could slow down or prevent you from achieving your goals, personally and professionally.
Write down the action steps that you must take to minimize the impact of each threat.

Chapter 21
Your Communication Strategy

"It is crucial that you speak to people in their emotional language so they will understand what you are saying."

Throughout my entire life, there has been one common theme that I have heard from many people, at many different levels of life and work: Failure in almost any relationship, in personal or professional life, takes place because of a lack of communication. Knowing this should be a big clue in life that you need to always work on improving your communication skills. It's why it is one of my four key Characteristics in my **Path to the Ultimate Life** visual. If you don't know how to openly communicate, you will find life is a struggle in many areas. You will not do well in relationships, friendships, job interviews, or proposals in business—just to name a few. You need to know how to share what is on your mind and how you feel.

If open communication is one of the biggest problems in life for people, and if YOU have a personal communication strategy, then you will have an advantage over all other people around you. If you are skilled in good communication, then I guarantee people will want to scream your name and beg for more.

As I stated in the chapter on the power of networking, we tend to communicate with people just like we are talking to someone who is just like us. That is an ineffective communication style. You are saying one thing, and they are hearing another because their personality and life experience filters are different than yours. It is important that you understand that everyone gives and receives information in very different styles. This is exactly why email and texting are not always the best means of communication. Both email and texting are emotionless, toneless methods of communication. You can't hear the tone of voice and you can't see the body language from the person sending the message. Because of this, your message just says what it says, and is open to a multitude of interpretations, which is why it can oftentimes come across

as cold or curt, and can be misinterpreted. What happens is
that the receiver of the text or email interprets what you are
trying to say through their own filter of beliefs and
experiences, and many times misinterprets the email or text
in a way that can create unnecessary conflict, anger, or hurt
feelings. They then fire off a response back, and now you
are in this firestorm of texts or emails.

Because of the possibility for misinterpretation, there
are a few things that you should never discuss or send over
email or texts. They are as follows:

Disagreements:

Never try to have a conversation over text or email on
a subject of disagreement. You typically respond out of
hurt or anger because of something that the other person
has said to defend their position. Because people feel much
bolder behind a phone or computer screen, they are usually
more willing to type in a much harsher statement than they
would if they were having the discussion with you face-to-
face. If you have a disagreement with someone, write down
the key items in bullet point format that you would like to
talk about, go somewhere public to keep both parties'
emotions in check, and have open, honest communication
about it.

Bad News:

This can be anything from resigning from a job, firing

someone, breaking up with someone, or relaying the news that a person has passed away. The bottom line is, don't send shock waves through someone's life by sending them the bad news over a text or email. That person woke up ready to rock the day, and then you decided to send them an email that, within seconds, could have a devastating impact on their life. Take the time to find someone else to go with you and deliver the news in-person. Think about what you will say, how you will say it, and the potential reaction of the person so you can help them deal with the news. Some situations, like firing a bad employee, you can't help very much, but you can still encourage them as they leave your company, by helping them to understand *why* they got fired. One of my favorites is the person who breaks up with someone via text. Listen, if you have been in a relationship with someone and have spent intimate moments with them connecting, then have the guts to stand before them and have a conversation with them about breaking up. If you don't have the strength to have that conversation, you are going to be very challenged in life because so many other conversations in life are much more difficult. Bottom line…if it is bad news, and the feelings that the other person is going to feel are hurt or anguish, do it face to face.

Negativity:

This is another huge no-no. Many friends and couples

get caught in this battleground when they are not on the same page or are having a disagreement. Because we are more aggressive communicators via text or email, we send hurtful statements that we would not normally send with the sole purpose of inflicting pain. These statements are like daggers being stuck into someone's chest, and you can't take that stuff back…it's in writing! If you have something negative that you feel about someone, take the steps to sit with them and talk it out.

Big News:

Now this one I can go halfway on. I think it's a big surprise when I get some exciting news over my text or email. It makes you jump for joy, but sometimes you leave the person all alone in the good news. I think it's okay to send big news via text or an email to surprise someone, but always follow up with a quick phone call to share in the excitement with them. People want to talk about big news, they want to scream your name and beg for more because you were there when they got it. I've sent many texts to my wife and kids saying, "Hey, guess what?" When they respond back "What?" I give them the news, and then call them a few seconds later. Texts and emails are great ways to set up a face to face or phone call to celebrate big news, but never leave it to just a text or email, that takes away from the excitement of the big news.

Let's talk for a bit about social media. I know that many reading this book probably think that social media is a bad thing in our society. You may be saying, "I don't do Facebook or Instagram, and I don't have a LinkedIn account." All I will say is, you are doing yourself and those around you a disservice by not using Facebook or LinkedIn as a communication tool.

What you need to understand about the various social media formats is that they expand your ability to network, reach out, create opportunities, and record some of your greatest moments in life. In this age of digital media, who looks through their photo albums, when you can click a button and check out what just happened in your friend's or family's life on Facebook, Instagram, or any other social media site. There is no way that any relative could know so much about their friends and family just by making phone calls. Facebook, Instagram, and other social media sharing tools allow you to see the exciting things going on in everyone's life that is important to you.

Many will say, "Well if they want to share it with me, they can just call me." That's impossible. From their end, they have a mother, father, two brothers, a sister, five aunts, five uncles, grandparents, twelve cousins, and who knows how many hundred friends. A person could make a full-time job out of sitting on the phone and calling everyone that they would love to share the things in their life with.

On your end, imagine all of those people I just

mentioned above, calling you to share great things happening in their life, as they happened. You would turn your phone off because you don't have the time for all of them to call. Programs like Facebook and Instagram allow you to participate in someone's life in a deep and intimate way when you can't be there in person and when it's convenient for you. There is no need to catch up at the annual family reunion like before, because you have seen your far away relative's baby take their first steps as it happened, your sister's son graduate high school and you were able to see your child's experiences at college. It's never as good as being there in person but you were able to live it out as it happened. I encourage you to embrace social technologies as a means to help you stay closer to the many people that you wish you had. You can share in their life events every day, versus looking back at a family reunion saying, "I wish I had more time to spend with them."

I am one of those people who uses my social media tools as a way to reach out and send encouraging messages to all of those who are connected to me. I personally use Facebook, LinkedIn, Instagram, Twitter, and Hootsuite. The combination of these programs allows me to reach thousands of people at my fingertips. Why is this important? I travel the country for business and I see many of the people face to face that are connected to me on social media. I have had many people tell me that they might have been having a bad day, when something I posted comes across their news feed on Facebook or LinkedIn, or a fun picture on Instagram, and it makes their day. It brightens the moment or lets them know that no matter what you are going through right now, it will be okay. Most people don't need a solution in the moment they just want to know that they aren't alone and that it will eventually be okay. My posts are all about making people know that they aren't alone in this thing called life, and that someone out there cares. Tap into your inner being and seek to reach people for good with social media.

I want to conclude this chapter by talking about some effective keys to communication. One of the biggest mistakes that I've witnessed, and that I'm guilty of, is people choosing to discuss something at the wrong time. Remember my story about walking in and seeing on the white board the three words that you need for effective communication: timing, intent, message. This is so true. There is a time, a tone, and a tact to communicating anything. I'm going to add a fourth word: expectations. So many times we set goals for the other person because we set in our minds how we believe we want them to react or respond to what we say. When they respond in a totally different way, we freak out. In the area of communication, you need to share your ideas and thoughts without any expectation as to how the other person is going to respond. Be ready for any response, though…not just the one you want to hear, because many times you won't.

When you go to discuss anything with anyone, always think through:

- Is this the right time?
- What is my intent in communicating this?
- What do I want them to hear?
- What are my expectations of them?

If you choose the right time, have good intentions, say your message in a way that they hear you without any real expectations of the outcome, you will most likely be very successful in getting what you want, or at least be at peace with how things turn out.

When it comes to the "right time" to talk about anything, I know there are a few moments in life that you don't ever want to talk about anything big, or get into a disagreement:

- When you are tired
- When you are hungry
- When you are angry
- Late at night

This is especially true in relationships and business dealings. More couples end up in huge arguments over the smallest things because one of them is pressing the other late at night. ...Bad move. Take a step back and say, "You know what, we shouldn't talk about this while we are tired. Let's sleep on it, and talk about it over breakfast." This allows the mind time to rest, and if it is a big deal, you will still want to talk about it in the morning when you are well-rested.

Regarding hungry and angry, well those speak for themselves. You just don't want to speak to someone about an issue when they are angry, especially when you really need to hear what is being said. Their minds aren't receptive. When people are hungry they can become irritated due to low blood sugar levels. In my house, we call this HANGRY. Take some time to sit down and do the following:

- Analyze who you are, to know and understand your communication style.
- Learn the various personality types from the networking chapter, to know how you need to address others.
- Always be thinking of the four questions that I mentioned in this chapter, on timing, intent, message, and expectations.
- Know when NOT to bring something of importance up.

If you work on those four key areas, you will learn to be a master communicator and grow the group of people screaming your name and begging for more throughout your life.

Application to the Ultimate Life

Describe your communication style.

Do you utilize the various social media programs? If not, why not? If so, how does it help in your relationships?

When communicating, which area do you struggle with the most: timing, intent, message, or expectation? Why?

What do you feel you need to improve on the most with regards to open communication?

Do you have the patience to live by the four rules of when NOT to talk about something of importance?

Action Steps to the Ultimate Life

When you feel negative emotions starting to rise up during any important conversation, take a step back, and request that you give the situation a 24-hour break before talking about it again.

The next time you have something important to talk to someone about, write down in bullet point format what you want to communicate.

Write down how you are feeling about what you want to communicate to someone.

Chapter 22
Be the Miracle!

"The more you are the miracle in other people's lives the more miraculous your life becomes."

For me, this is one of the most important chapters for you to grasp, from a philosophical perspective. There are a lot of qualities that you need to have in order to get people to scream your name and beg for more, but there's one quality that will keep them away or make them stay close...let's talk about it:

If you are going to leverage the people you meet in life, you need to be seen as a giver, not a taker when dealing with them. Have you ever been around a taker? Their "What's in it for me" radar is always on when they are around. The questions they ask and the actions they take tell you that anything they say, ask, or do for you is all in an effort to get something in return. They aren't about giving anything to you, and people pick up on this very quickly.

People who are givers, with expectation of nothing in return, get more "YES" than "NO" in life because people see them in a very different light. Do you get "NO" in a lot of your requests of parents, friends, or business colleagues for things that others are getting a "YES" to? If so, you need to take a serious look at this area. Do you say "NO" to requests often? Or, are you constantly asking for favors or requests without ever offering up help. Remember the story about the young White House intern, who worked her way up the ladder by simply asking one question to everyone she met…"How can I help you?" People remember those people, especially if they make a request and you pull it off for them. You are a hero, and they tell others about you.

I love watching the movie, *Bruce Almighty*, because it sets up this very concept. It actually was life-changing for me the moment I saw it years ago. I was one of those people who saw the talents I had and I believed I could be great in whatever industry I worked. As I shared my own personality traits earlier, I was a "start everything, finish nothing" kind of person. I went at everyone in an effort to help myself be successful, and that attitude didn't work very well. Like Bruce Almighty, I was always praying for a big break…praying for it to walk right into my hands…praying for life to open up, and all my talents and great ideas to take shape. Then one night, I watched Bruce Almighty, and I heard GOD, played by Morgan Freeman, say to Bruce, "Stop praying for a miracle and be the miracle."

As they say on Facebook, "OMG!" A revelation came flying through my soul. Going back to my **Path to the Ultimate Life** visual, I had to change the choices I was making. By changing my choices, it had a profound impact on my decisions with people, money, and time. The choice that I made was to "Be the MIRACLE" in other people's lives, by focusing in on their needs, wants, and desires as I spoke to or interacted with them. I paid attention to the things that they said seemed to be obstacles, or that were keeping them from reaching their dreams and purpose. As I listened, I would offer input or seek to connect them with someone that I knew who could help them. As this began to happen, I began to become more welcoming to people. I saw people's lives reach new levels because they were introduced to someone by me who could help make their life better. Don't think that miracles have to be huge. Sometimes it is as simple as helping someone with a seemingly small problem in your mind, but in the context of where that person is in life, helping them find the solution to that "small thing" is a huge deal for that person.

   A great story that I think about in this context was with a vendor that we used to have several years ago. I became a close business associate of this person over the years and I worked with him to better understand our industry because I wanted his product to be the best for everyone. If it was the best for everyone, then it would be the best for our company as well. After being involved with the product for a couple of months, I knew that they were on the right track. As we were talking at a conference, he indicated that he was really looking to go to the next level with his company. I really believed in his vision for the company, and being in his late twenties, I wanted to see him be a major player in our industry. I leaned over to him and said, "Look, here's the deal. I believe in you, your team, and your product. If you have any clients who are on the fence in the sales process, you give them my email and number and have them call me. I'll take care of the rest." The look in his eyes was amazement. He was like, "Really? You would do that? How much do I have to pay you in a finder's fee?" My answer: "Nothing. I want to see you do well, and I want my recommendation to be pure, not paid for. Just continue the incredible service and product development that you are doing in your company." I proceeded to take calls over the next few years from potential clients, and within a thirty-minute conversation, slammed the door on the competition for them. A number

of years later, he landed a nice payday by selling his
company to an affiliated company, who was looking to get
into his line of work. This was a big day for him in his life.
He called me up after the sale and thanked me for being a
huge influence on the clients that put him in a position to
sell his company. That's being a miracle for someone…
reaching out, seizing the moment, and using your talents
and time to create life-changing moments for others…with
no expectation in return.

One more example of "being the miracle" and then
we'll move on. I'm pretty active on some industry online
forums. I often look through my email notices from people
who need basic information, who seek a connection to
someone who will help them with a problem, or to open up
an opportunity. I take the time each day to respond to one
or two people. I consistently get emails back thanking me
for my connection or insight, as it helped save them a ton
of time or money. Making a difference and helping doesn't
have to take much time or money, it just takes you reaching
out and listening.

Never underestimate how big of a deal a problem or
opportunity is for someone. What might seem simple or
small to you may be a huge deal in that moment to them
because of the huge checklist of things on their to-do list, or
because other people may be putting pressure on them in
life. If you are continuing to expand your network of
people listed in your phone, then leverage that network to

help those that you come into contact with. This one step alone will cause people to scream your name and beg for more because you will have become the ultimate connector in their life.

You may be asking, "Why be the miracle? I don't like people that much." What I will ask, is for you to remember that feeling when someone reached out to you and took the time to be the miracle in your life. You were in a place where nothing seemed to go right. You were trying everything in your own strength to change your direction, and you felt like your path was riddled with bottomless pits that you kept falling into. Then someone came into your life at that very moment, pulled you out of the pit, gave you a solution or introduced you to a solution, or, they just helped you. They walked you around the bottomless pits to the other side of a straight and safe road towards your goal. That feeling of relief was amazing, wasn't it? The internal feeling of excitement from knowing that the situation is gone and you can breathe again is incredible. You feel FREE again, and are back on the path to good choices…to reaching your goals in life.

Knowing how good it feels when someone reaches out to you should cause you to want to be the same "miracle" to others who come into your life with the same type of anxiety and challenges. Everyone has talents, experiences, and a network of people that others can benefit from. You need to take a mental inventory of what those are so you can easily identify when people around you need help.

One thing I want to stress at this point is in my **Path to the Ultimate Life** visual: as you make a CHOICE to be the miracle to others, it will impact your TIME. You can get caught up in saying "YES" to too many people, and it dominates your time, thus preventing you from staying on path to meet your goals and purpose. This is where you need to make a second CHOICE, to learn when to say, "I can't help right now because my glass is full." Learn to know when your glass of energy, emotional presence, and time are full, so you know when to say "no." If you allow your glass of energy, emotional presence, and time to overrun for too long, your attitude will begin to be seen as negative, because you have no PARTY time. You need a way to refresh yourself and to help you stay on track towards your goal of the ultimate life.

Are you beginning to see how the various things that I'm talking about in the book are interconnected? Just by making a choice to be more giving of your time and network could impact your choices, time, money, people, purpose, and party elements. Be wise with them in order to stay on the path toward getting people to scream your name and beg for more so you achieve the ultimate life.

Application to the Ultimate Life

Do you like to help people? Why or why not?
What are the challenges that prevent you from reaching out to people around you who are in need?
What issues are going on in your life that are keeping you from being the miracle for others?
When looking at your choices, money, time, and people, which one do you think you need to focus on in order to be the miracle for others?

Action Steps to the Ultimate Life

Write down your own story about when someone that you didn't expect reached out and helped you with a challenge or opportunity.
Make a commitment to try and be the miracle for at least two people each month. Look for the "low-hanging fruit on the tree." These are people whose needs you can easily help, without dominating your time.

Chapter 23
Narrow Your Focus...Dominate Your Space

"When your life glass of time is overflowing, you have a mess in your life. Learn to narrow your focus and keep your glass of time from spilling everywhere."

As you may have learned throughout this book, up until my early 30's I was a "start everything" kind of idea guy. I was all over the place looking for that "thing" that could take me to the promise land, make me rich, and accelerate my progress through the stages of life...from entry level management to super-star status, or even early retirement. I was looking for the shortcuts, without all the hard work that comes with obtaining long-term success.

What I have learned is, if you continue to grab for every idea that comes along in your mind, you will spread yourself thin mentally and experience utter frustration over feeling like a failure at never getting traction in any of your ideas. One of the challenges that I think many young people suffer from is the fact they have lived through the growth of the dot com age of technology, where many bright, and not so bright people in their early to mid-twenties hit it huge with some type of technology development. Because of that, as well as being told their entire life that they were as good as the best on the team, without any proof of their performance or actually earning those accolades, they have looked for the easy route to the good life, believing that they deserved it without hard work and persistence.

I'm here to tell you that most people don't achieve the quality of life that they want without hard work and paying close attention to the four Pillars and Characteristics I talk about in my **Path to the Ultimate Life** visual. If you are going to achieve success with your goals in life, it is important that you follow the path that I have laid out throughout this book, to discover the things that I have shared in this book like your purpose, passion, priorities, and principles. These will help to keep you focused on the prize of life that you desire. The more you run from one idea to the next, the more you will be like a ball in a pin ball machine, bouncing all over the place until one day, you land in the hole. A few key questions to be asking yourself in order to stay focused are:

- What am I good at?
- What are my strengths?
- What do I want to achieve?
- What do I like doing?
- What people do I want to help?

Asking these questions will help you to define what you would like to do in life. As you determine where you want to go, with the end game in mind, you stay focused on that goal. As we talked in the chapter on threats, you don't let anything deter you from that goal. If it's important enough for you and where you want to go in life, nothing should get in the way of it.

With that being said, I want to step back a moment and warn you not to let a goal become an idol in your life to the point where you rule out the most important people around you because of your pursuit of it. It happens every day. This is where your priorities are connected to your pursuit. If your family is your most important priority, then you don't become obsessed by working late due to your goal. Doing this means that you have elevated your work life as your number one priority, and you had committed in your plan to make your family your number one priority. Remember, financial security is a big deal for a family, but quality time is an even bigger deal. You need to find that balance.

If you are a college student and you want to find that first, nice entry-level job, then you can't let the distractions on campus and potential relationships get in the way. That's not to say that you don't have fun in college. Live it up, but make your studies your top priority. You will be glad you did when you are in your post-college interviews, and the HR Director or President of the company asks you, "So what was your GPA?" What you say next will determine whether your interview goes any further. If finding a great offer out of college is not your goal, and you just want to have a great time in school and get a degree with say, a 2.2 GPA, then go for it, and do it with all your might. However, hear me on this: You have just selected the long route to a great paying job. Employers look at your GPA and say to themselves, "They had all the time in the world to work hard and study, and they didn't make the grades. What makes me think that they will work hard here at our company?" Once an employer is asking those questions, your interview is over. Your GPA says to them whether or not you are a hard worker.

Let me take a quick, little side tangent for college students on the topic of relationships. I'm all for you going out with people in college. Have a blast. Get to know tons of people. However, when it comes to dating, I'm an advocate of not committing to a serious one-on-one relationship in college, for a couple of very specific reasons.

First, you will miss out on so much of the college experience. There is so much that goes on in college that having an exclusive relationship will hold you back from experiencing. You will stop going to many exciting college events because you will begin to separate yourself, staying at your place, hanging out together, thinking that the world now ends with the both of you. I'm here to tell you, the world outside your room on your college campus is passing you by. College is the time to build the network of people around you. Get out and be a part of extra-curricular activities because one day in the future, those people that you meet are going to be Presidents of companies, Vice Presidents of departments, and influential people in the economy of your life. Once you leave college, all of those people will eventually be in a great place in life, and the one thing that will get you in the door to see them is that you are alumni, a fraternity brother, a sorority sister, or you have some other common bond that you were able to establish in college. When you pick one person in college that you choose to exclusively hang out with, you put yourself at a personal disadvantage for the future.

Another big reason for this mindset is that everyone you meet in college is going to mature into different people over the next eight to ten years after graduation. Many of them will mature into someone who you wouldn't even give the time of day had you known how they were going to mature. I encourage all college students to make college your playground for learning about yourself and others. Then use that experience and knowledge once you graduate to find the person that you want to spend the rest of your life with. I've seen so many young people who were great students in the classroom, but had a horrible work ethic in the workplace. The bad time to find this out is a year into your marriage because you dated early, got engaged your senior year, and married right out of college.

Take your time. There is nothing wrong with waiting and enjoying life; learn who you are and let those you might want to build a life with you grow up, so you get a sense of what you are getting into. The bottom line is: the emotional ups and downs of a young relationship can be a huge threat to you achieving your goals and the ultimate life you want in college. Make a wise choice.

Now for all of you out of college the same holds true when running your business, having a successful marriage, moving up your career ladder, and in just "doing life." If you look at a glass as the amount of time that you have to give to everything that you are going to commit to in daily life, you only have so much to give. Once your glass is full, it's full. If your glass begins to run over because of over committing, then everything inside the glass will start to run out, and you will have a mess everywhere. You will begin to feel overburdened, overworked, and burnt out. You've become distracted from your purpose, you've lost your passion, your priorities are out of order, and you stopped having the "party" that refreshes your "glass of energy" because there isn't any room or time to enjoy it. You have lost your focus. That is why it is so important to narrow your focus on the things that are the most important to you and to dominate your space.

Guard the amount of energy, emotions, and time that you commit to, so that you don't become average at anything. Whatever and whomever you commit to, you want to do it AWESOME! If you continually pull off awesome for people, they will love to scream your name and beg for more.

Application to the Ultimate Life

What distractions keep you from being able focus on your purpose?
What are the top three things that you need to rule out of your life in order to get focused on your life?
In the area of choices, money, people, or time: which ones do you feel you need to refocus on in order to achieve your goals in life?
What would you like to be great at?

Action Steps to the Ultimate Life

Write down three things you are going to rule out of your life in order to help you bring clarity and focus to your goals.

Buy a written planner or use the one on your mobile device to start writing down the things that you need to do daily, to narrow your focus and achieve your goals.

Ask a close friend, who has a very organized life to chat with you about how they stay focused on their goals.

Chapter 24
The Three Questions

"Failure to learn the lessons of your mistakes will allow you to keep making the same mistake over and over. Never be afraid to ask the right questions about your life."

With every plan in life, whether personal or professional, there are three questions that you must ask of yourself on a consistent basis. These three questions ensure you are on target with your goals, as close to the time frame that you wanted, and that you expose the gaps in your progress so you can make some immediate changes and not get side-tracked and off course.

It is important that you ask these questions about each area of the **Path to the Ultimate Life** visual. If you are to make positive change towards your goals and purpose in life, then you will need to fine-tune and make some big and small changes in some or all eight of the areas of this visual.

The three questions that you need to ask in each area are:

- What am I CURRENTLY doing that I need to do differently?
- What am I NOT doing that I need to start doing?
- What am I doing that I need to STOP because it isn't relevant?

It is important that you ask these three questions in the following intervals:

- Before you pursue your plan, make sure you start with good execution.
- Quarterly, in the first year, ensure that you make good progress.
- At least annually, make adjustments given changes that will occur in your life.

I've put my **Path to the Ultimate Life** visual on the next page, along with the key areas that you will need to think through, as well as the three questions for each part of the visual. This is a chapter about self-reflection and thinking through your life. You can choose to take the time to work through this in-depth and then read the last chapter, or read the last chapter, and then come back to it.

This entire book has been helping you to think through the key areas of your life leading up to this moment, when you will put the pieces of your life puzzle together.

Take time to analyze each area, and either write your responses in this book, or if there isn't enough room, write up a document that you can keep on your mobile device so you can refer to it at anytime. I prefer that you write it in a document that you can refer to on your mobile device. It's your life plan. It's worth having with you at all times.

Good luck with your life analysis.

Your Action Plan to the Ultimate Life

What is your PURPOSE in life?

What is your PASSION in life?

What are six core PRINCIPLES that you are going to live by?

1.

2.

3.

4.

5.

6.

Describe the key characteristics of the type of PEOPLE that you want to surround yourself with?

1.

2.

3.

4.

5.

6.

What organizations or networks of people must you become involved with in order to meet these types of people?

1.

2.

3.

4.

5.

Put the following PRIORITIES in the order that you want to live by. Add others in the extra space if you have any. If some don't apply to your life, mark NA on them. They may apply at some point in your future.

____ Spouse/Partner
____ Other Family
____ Work
____ Education
____ Personal Fulfillment
____ Volunteering (church/nonprofit work)
____ Children
____ Friends

_____ Faith or Spiritual Beliefs
_____ Personal Health

_____ _____

_____ _____

_____ _____

What three things in your PAST must you forgive, accept, or let go of in order for you to embrace all that the future has for you?

1.

2.

3.

What is your "PARTY" that you are going to put on your schedule at least once a week so you can consistently refresh your energy and passion in life?

Choices:

What am I doing now that I need to do differently?

What am I not doing that I need to start doing?

What am I doing that I need to stop because it's no longer relevant?

Time:

What am I doing now that I need to do differently?

What am I not doing that I need to start doing?

What am I doing that I need to stop doing because it's no longer relevant?

Money:

What am I doing now that I need to do differently?

What am I not doing that I need to start doing?

What am I doing that I need to stop because it's no longer relevant?

People:

What am I doing now that I need to do differently?

What am I not doing that I need to start doing?

What am I doing that I need to stop because it's no longer relevant?

Attitude:

What am I doing now that I need to do differently?

What am I not doing that I need to start doing?

What am I doing that I need to stop because it's no longer relevant?

Communication:

What am I doing now that I need to do differently?

What am I not doing that I need to start doing?

What am I doing that I need to stop because it's no longer relevant?

Ability to Adapt:

What am I doing now that I need to do differently?

What am I not doing that I need to start doing?

What am I doing that I need to stop because it's no longer relevant?

Perseverance:

What am I doing now that I need to do differently?

What am I not doing that I need to start doing?

What am I doing that I need to stop because it's no longer relevant?

The ONLY thing that will hold you back from obtaining everything that you want in life is YOU.

Chapter 25
You Can't Escape Your Legacy

"Your legacy will live on for generations. Will it be good or bad? You get to choose."

Wow! I can't believe that our time is coming to a close. I can't believe that we have spent so much time together over the last twenty-four chapters, working through every aspect of what seeking the ultimate life can be for you. It's hard to bring things to a close. I've shared with you many of my stories, challenges, and the things that I have learned in life. You have looked deep into your life, shared the things that you want to change about your life, and built a plan to succeed...which is awesome. I appreciate you being open and honest with yourself. You have established a path to achieve the things that you want in life that are going to have a lasting impact on your life, as well as all of those around you, including your family, kids, and friends.

Whether you like it or not, you will have a legacy. No one gets to escape it. Your legacy is going to either be good or bad. The image that you leave behind is either good or bad. The memories that you leave behind with your kids, grandkids, family, and close friends are either going to be good or bad. Your legacy is what you leave behind. Some people reading this book only need to make slight changes in order to leave behind a legacy for their children and grandchildren that would make them proud. Others need to make big changes in their life and to break the generational curse of struggle that has plagued their life. I recall an interview that I heard once from a well-known boxer, who was asked by the reporter, "You are vicious in the ring, like a raging tiger, who is angry. Where does that emotion come from?" He replied, "I hated my father and the way he treated me as I grew up. Every time I get into the ring, it's my time to get even with him." As a father, I feel for him because he has this huge hole in his soul and a longing for his parent to love him. He wants to carry on his father's legacy, but he can't because of the amount of pain that goes with it. Many people carry that same pain from someone in our life for whom we cared deeply. For many, it is their parents. If you are on the path of leaving a painful legacy behind and want to change, YOU CAN! Hope is in your plan that you have thought through in this book.

No matter what your age, your children will one day carry your legacy with them into the future. Is your legacy one that can empower and build their life? Or, is it going to be a legacy that they will struggle with for years? I'm asking these questions because I want you to think about your legacy as you begin to pursue your goals and enhancing your quality of life.

Winston Churchill once said, "We make a living by what we get. We make a life by what we give." I encourage you to be a giver of life, not a taker. If you give all around you, life will come to you in ways that you never thought possible because giving is like a magnet…It draws people to you.

People are looking for H.O.P.E. all around them. To me, H.O.P.E. is a great acronym for:

- **H**ell of an attitude.
- **O**ptimistic.
- **P**assionate.
- **E**nergetic.

Seek to be a person who brings a positive attitude,

optimism, passion, and energy to those you come in contact with each day. Remember, anything worth doing is worth doing with all your might. Keep a copy of the **Path to the Ultimate Life** visual on your mobile device. Focus on the four Pillars in your decision-making process. Improve on the four Characteristics needed in order to do the four Pillars with excellence. Pay attention to your threats. Work your life plan. Expand your network of people continually. Keep your legacy in mind as you flow through life. Most importantly, as you touch people's lives, be a giver of life.

Thank you for sharing your time with me in this incredible journey. As you look at what tomorrow will bring, GO BIG, GO BOLD, AND GO NOW! You will never regret making the decision to improve your life and chase your dreams.

Path To The Ultimate Life ™

Attitude

Communication

Perseverance

Ability to Adapt

Acknowledgements

I am so blessed to have had so many people come through my path in life that have taught me so many lessons that shaped my life. I have so many memories with these people. I'm very thankful for social media that allows us to express our fun-filled lives to others and help encourage them to be better than their circumstances. I'm also thankful for social media, in that it allows us to reflect in both words and pictures and appreciate the amazing lives we have with the people and experiences surrounding us.

First, I would like to thank all of my industry friends across the country, in the Florida Society of Association Executives, American Society of Association Executives, and the Council of Manufacturing Associations. Business is boring if you aren't creating friends in the industry. The relationships, friendships and life-long memories you have helped me create in my life that I have drawn from are incredible. Thank you for giving me life each year.
I would like to thank my family who, throughout my life, has helped create and provide me with stories and life lessons that have made this book possible. Growing up was a fun-filled experience with my aunts, uncles, cousins and brother.

I would like to thank my parents Jeanette and Charlie who have sowed so much into my life. Dad, thank you for sharing how a man can care, have compassion, and show understanding. Thank you for being willing to be firm in your words and discipline to keep me focused on making good choices. Mom, thank you for giving me the drive to be successful and a natural-born energy to enjoy life every day. I'm proud to be your son and call you my mom and dad.

To my kids and their spouses, I have so much to say and so little room. Thomas and Kristin, Brittany and Joseph, Kristen and Garrett… You are all an inspiration to me as young adults. Your love and compassion for people and the direction you have chosen for your life are exciting. Thank you for being such awesome children, young adults, spouses, and SSD's (super step-daughters)! And remember… "Make Good Choices!"

To the most important person in my life, my wife DeAnna, I would like to say, THANK YOU, for being such an amazing support and encourager in my life. You are amazing to wake up to, live life with, and go to sleep with every day. You have been the number one inspiration of this book and thank you for pushing me to write it. I love you forever.

Lastly, I would like to thank God for giving me the inspiration and words to write this book. Thank you for having the strength above mine to pull off such amazing things during my life. Thank you for always being there for me to handle the smallest of details and to make the biggest miracles happen.

Author Bio

Tom Morrison is a 1990
graduate of Florida State
University with a B.S. in
Finance. He began his
career in association
management in 1995 as an
Executive Vice President
hired to assume the role of
CEO of the Florida

Automotive Industry Association. Tom lead FAIA to be
recognized as one of the top 10 influences in the $260
billion automotive aftermarket in 1998.

In late 2005, Tom was hired by the Metal Treating Institute
as Executive Vice President to assume the role of CEO of
MTI Management in 2008. Tom has been instrumental in
helping MTI drive growth in their member value
proposition, trade show, annual conferences, online
technical training, and use of technology. Through Tom's
leadership, MTI has grown to be one of the top
manufacturing associations in the United States.

Tom is active in the Florida Society of Association
Executives, Council of Manufacturing Associations, and
American Society of Association Executives. In 2012, due
to peer recognition of Tom's professionalism, business

innovation, and passion, he was named the FSAE Association Executive of the Year.

Tom has been published in the numerous national publications including, *The Source Magazine*, *Associations Now* in the association field, and most recently recognized as a case study in the book, *The Art of Membership* by Shari Jacobs.

In addition to running a full-time association, Tom enjoys speaking to groups about association growth, finding their passions, and maximizing their quality of life. Due to his recognition as an extremely knowledgeable industry veteran, and his engaging, highly energetic delivery, he is a much sought-after speaker. He educates people on how to create and deliver high value and passion, making "believers" of association members, helping to create financial security for associations, and how to achieve the ultimate quality of life.

Tom lives in Jacksonville, Florida with his wife DeAnna, who is an ACE Certified Personal Trainer and an ACE Certified Health Coach, and their three grown children.

Twitter: @tommorrison
Website: ScreamYourNameBook.com
Facebook: Facebook.com/ScreamYourNameBook

Reference Page

America Psychology Association: 190
Bruce Almighty – Movie: 252
Gallop: 190
Dr. John Van Epp: 208
Dr. Richard Marks: 208
National Center for Educational Statistics: 190
National Center for Health Statistics: 173
Social Security Office or Research and Statistics: 154
U.S. Census Bureau: 226
Webster's Dictionary: 67, 88, 205
Zig Ziglar: 75